# SELF-DIRECTED LEARNING

# SELF-DIRECTED LEARNING

*A Guide for Learners and Teachers*

MALCOLM S. KNOWLES

**CAMBRIDGE** Adult Education
Prentice Hall Regents, Englewood Cliffs, NJ 07632

SELF-DIRECTED LEARNING

Copyright © 1975 by Malcolm S. Knowles

Published and distributed by:

**CAMBRIDGE** Adult Education
Prentice Hall Regents, Englewood Cliffs, NJ 07632

ISBN   0-8428-2215-1

Prentice-Hall International (UK) Limited, *London*
Prentice-Hall of Australia Pty. Limited, *Sydney*
Prentice-Hall Canada Inc., *Toronto*
Prentice-Hall Hispanoamericana, S.A., *Mexico*
Prentice-Hall of India Private Limited, *New Delhi*
Prentice-Hall of Japan, Inc., *Tokyo*
Simon & Schuster Asia Pte. Ltd., *Singapore*
Editora Prentice-Hall do Brasil, Ltda., *Rio de Janeiro*

**Library of Congress Cataloging in Publication Data**

Knowles, Malcolm Shepherd, 1913–
  The modern practice of adult education.

  Bibliography: p.
  Includes index.
  1. Adult education.   I. Title.
LC5215.K62   1980      374      80-14344
ISBN 0-8428-2215-1

# Contents

Orientation ............................... 7

**PART I—THE LEARNER**

For the Learner ............................ 9

> Setting a Climate, 9
> Diagnosing Needs for Learning, 11
> Designing a Learning Plan, 12
> Inquiry Project No. 1, 14
> Inquiry Project No. 2, 18
> Inquiry Project No. 3, 23
> Inquiry Project No. 4, 25

**PART II—THE TEACHER**

For the Teacher ........................... 29

> Setting a Climate, 29
> Defining a New Role, 31
> Developing Self-Directed Learners, 39
> Implementing the Role of Facilitator, 44

**PART III—LEARNING RESOURCES**

General ................................. 59

    A. *Comparison of Assumptions*
       *and Processes, 60*

    B. *Competencies of Self-Directed Learning, 61*

    C. *Learning Contact, 62*

Climate Setting and Relationship Building ...... 64

    D. *The Self-Concept of a Self-Directing*
       *Person, 64*

    E. *Relationship Building Exercises, 71*

    F. *Consultation Skill-Practice Exercise, 75*

Diagnosing Learning Needs .................. 81

    G. *Self-Assessment Exercise, 81*

    H. *A Content-Course Self-Assessment*
       *Instrument, 92-93*

Formulating Objectives ...................... 94

    I. *Some Guidelines for Stating Objectives, 94*

Using Learning Strategies and Resources ........ 99

    J. *Questioning Strategies and Techniques, 99*

    K. *Relating Methods to Objectives, 104*

    L. *Exercise in Reading a Book Proactively, 105*

    M. *Exercise in Using Human Resources*
       *Proactively, 108*

Evaluation ............................... 110

    N. *Types of Evidence for Different*
       *Objectives, 110*

    O. *Some Examples of Rating Scales, 112*

Appendix—Guidelines for Contract Learning .... 129

# Orientation

As the book's subtitle states, this book is designed to be used by both learners and teachers. The results will be best if it is used by them together. In such case, it would be helpful if each of them read both Parts I and II, so as to understand in advance their respective roles. Then the initiative may be taken by either party: the learners can suggest actions the teacher might take, and the teacher can suggest actions the learners might take.

But learners can use the book as a resource for developing their own competence as self-directed inquirers, in which case it still would be a good idea for them to read both Part I and Part II, and in the latter, simply substitute a "helper of any kind" for the word *teacher*. And teachers can use the book alone as a resource for designing strategies for helping their students learn how to take more responsibility for their own learning.

In any case, you will soon discover that this is not a book to be read and reacted to. It is a resource for you to use as a self-directed learner, whether you are a student or a teacher.

*Make it work for you!*

# PART I
# THE LEARNER

## For the Learner

Welcome to an adventure in self-directed learning. I'd like to start off by setting a climate for our mutual inquiry.

### Setting a Climate

First, I'd like it to be a warm climate. I'd like for you to feel that I care about you, even though I don't know you. At least you know that I care enough to take quite a bit of time to figure out how, without being able to see you, I can help you become a self-directed learner. I hope that you will feel warmly toward me, too, as you get to know me better through what I say.

Second, I'd like it to be a climate of mutual respect. I respect you for being interested enough in becoming a more self-directed learner to be willing to read this book. And I respect the experience and creativity you bring to this inquiry that will enable you to mold the ideas and suggestions in this book to your own needs and style. I hope you'll respect me for attempting something I have never done before—trying to help people become self-directed learners through the printed word.

Third, I'd like it to be a climate conducive to dialogue. I'd like you to feel free to participate actively in this inquiry, both by raising questions about what I say and supplying your own answers, and by following your own curiosities wherever they lead you. I would feel especially good if you are engaging in this inquiry along with others, with whom you can share the dialogue face to face.

Fourth, I'd like it to be a climate in which we are clear about, and secure in, our respective roles. I see my role to be that of a guide for, and facilitator of, your inquiry, as well as being a source of information about facts, ideas, and other forms of help. I shall try to be as skillful as possible in suggesting procedures for you to use in your inquiry, and I hope that these will not come through to you as impositions of my will on yours. Instead, I see your role as being an active inquirer and wanting to learn all you can from the resources I can provide—but on your terms, at your speed, and in your own style. I see you as accepting or rejecting ideas because they do or do not have meaning to you and not because I or someone else says you should. I hope you feel secure in taking this degree of responsibility, and I'll give you all the support I can.

Fifth and finally, I'd like to set a climate of mutual trust. Perhaps the most important condition for your being able to trust me is that I should be open and honest with you about my motives and biases. Regarding my motives, I have been so impressed with the joy that most of my students have found in self-directed learning (and the results they have achieved!) that I want to spread the gospel. My motives are the motives of a missionary—so beware, I'll try to convert you. And therein lies also my main bias—at least the main bias that I am aware of: *I think that self-directed learning is the best way to learn.* I acknowledge that there are situations in which teaching, instruction, and even indoctrination are called for. But I also think that every act of teaching should have built into it some provision for helping the learner become more self-directing. I recognize that there are situations in which a person is indeed dependent in some respects, and that in these situations it is appropriate for him or her to be taught or directed. But I don't think that it is healthy—or even humane—for a person to be kept permanently dependent upon a system or upon another person. I hope that this confession of my motives and biases will help you to trust me. As for my trusting you, I have faith that you will enter into this inquiry with an open mind, and that you will seriously consider the concepts and suggestions. But I also have faith that you will test them against your own value system, personality style, and experience, and will either reject or adapt those that don't stack up.

### Diagnosing Needs for Learning

Presumably, since you are reading this little book, you have become aware of a general need to at least find out something about self-directed learning. I can imagine that this might be true if you have recently had a belittling experience with an arrogant teacher or even a frustrating experience with a sloppy and disorganized teacher; or if you have entered into one of the nontraditional study programs that are flourishing around the country and have found yourself given more responsibility for your own learning than you were prepared for; or if you started out to learn something by yourself and fell flat on your face; or if you read somewhere that it is the "new thing," and simply became curious about what it's all about. Inquiry Project No. 1 is designed to investigate this basic need or curiosity further and to deepen your understanding of why self-directed learning may be important to you.

If this notion intrigues you, you might wish to turn to Inquiry Project No. 1 right now; if not, put it on the back burner to be looked at later if it becomes interesting.

In either case, it probably would be helpful for you to diagnose your needs to learn about self-directed learning at a more specific level. Inquiry Project No. 2 presents a definition of self-directed learning and the assumptions on which it is based. Inquiry Project No. 3 presents an overview of the competencies required to do it, thus providing a possible model for you to compare yourself to. You will want to test this model to determine what aspects of it make sense to you. Then I think you will find it useful to assess which of these aspects of the model you need to work on further—that is, which competencies need strengthening in order for you to become a more self-directing learner. Learning Resource B will help you do this. I suggest that at this point you might experiment with filling out the first column, "Learning Objectives," of a learning contract as illustrated in Learning Resource C. In this column you should list the learning objectives (about self-directed learning) that have emerged from Inquiry Project No. 3.

### Designing a Learning Plan

You are now ready to tackle Inquiry Project No. 4, which suggests strategies and resources for improving your competencies in self-directed learning. You can fill out columns 2, 3, and 4 of the learning contract as you engage in Inquiry Project No. 4.

Executing the learning activities is really Inquiry Project No. 5, but it is not in the book, since it consists of whatever your learning contract specifies, along with whatever help from teachers, other resource experts, and peers that it calls for. Evaluating your learning, which is the concluding phase of the self-directed learning process, is provided for in your learning contract.

*Happy adventuring.*

# Inquiry Project No. 1:
# Why Self-Directed Learning?

It is a tragic fact that most of us only know how to be taught; we haven't learned how to learn. Why is this a tragic fact? There are both immediate and long-run reasons.

One immediate reason is that there is convincing evidence that people who take the initiative in learning (proactive learners) learn more things, and learn better, than do people who sit at the feet of teachers passively waiting to be taught (reactive learners). (For definitions of proactive and reactive learners, see Learning Resource L.) They enter into learning more purposefully and with greater motivation. They also tend to retain and make use of what they learn better and longer than do the reactive learners.

A second immediate reason is that self-directed learning is more in tune with our natural processes of psychological development. When we are born we are totally dependent personalities. We need parents to protect us, feed us, carry us, and make decisions for us. But as we grow and mature we develop an increasingly deep psychological need to be independent, first, of parental control, and then, later, of control by teachers and other adults. An essential aspect of maturing is developing the ability to take increasing responsibility for our own lives—to become increasingly self-directing.

A third immediate reason is that many of the new developments in education—the new curriculums, open classrooms, nongraded schools, learning resource centers, independent study, nontraditional study programs, external degree programs, universities-without-walls, and the like—put a heavy responsibility on the learners to take a good deal of initiative in their own learning. Students entering into these programs without having learned the skills of self-directed inquiry will experience anxiety, frustration, and often failure, and so will their teachers. The rapid spread of this problem in high schools, technical institutes, community colleges, colleges and universities, and adult education is precisely what has caused this book to be written.

But there is also a long-run reason why it is tragic that we have not learned how to learn without being taught, and it is probably more important than all of the immediate reasons put together. Alvin Toffler calls this reason "future shock." The simple truth is that we are entering into a strange new world in which rapid change will be the only stable characteristic. And this simple truth has several radical implications for education and learning.

For one thing, this implies that it is no longer realistic to define the purpose of education as transmitting what is known. In a world in which the half-life of many facts (and skills) may be ten years or less, half of what a person has acquired at the age of twenty may be obsolete by the time that person is thirty. Thus, the main purpose of education must now be to develop the skills of inquiry. When a person leaves schooling he or she must not only have a

foundation of knowledge acquired in the course of learning to inquire but, more importantly, also have the ability
to go on acquiring new knowledge easily and skillfully
the rest of his or her life.

A second implication is that there must be a somewhat
different way of thinking about learning. Typically, we
think of learning as what takes place in school—it is
"being taught." To be adequate for our strange new world
we must come to think of learning as being the same as
living. We must learn from everything we do; we must
exploit every experience as a "learning experience." Every
institution in our community—government agency, store,
recreational organization, church—becomes a resource for
learning, as does every person we have access to—parent,
child, friend, service provider, doctor, teacher, fellow
worker, supervisor, minister, store clerk, and so on and
on. Learning means making use of every resource—in or
out of educational institutions—for our personal growth
and development.

A third implication is that it is no longer appropriate
to equate education with youth. In the civilization of our
forefathers it may have been possible for people to learn
in their youthful years most of what they would need to
know for the rest of their life, but this is no longer true.
Education—or, even better, learning—must now be defined as a lifelong process. The primary learning during
youth will be the skills of inquiry and the learning after
schooling is done will be focused on acquiring the knowledge, skills, understanding, attitude, and values required
for living adequately in a rapidly changing world.

To sum up: the "why" of self-directed learning is survival—your own survival as an individual, and also the
survival of the human race. Clearly, we are not talking
here about something that would be nice or desirable;

neither are we talking about some new educational fad. We are talking about a basic human competence—the ability to learn on one's own—that has suddenly become a prerequisite for living in this new world.

### RESOURCES FOR ADDITIONAL INQUIRY

Brown, George I. *Human Teaching for Human Learning.* New York: The Viking Press, 1971.

Eble, Kenneth E. *A Perfect Education.* New York: The Macmillan Co., 1968.

Faure, Edgar, and others. *Learning to Be: The World of Education Today and Tomorrow.* Paris: UNESCO, 1972.

Postman, Neil, and C. Weingartner. *Teaching as a Subversive Activity.* New York: Delacorte Press, 1969.

# Inquiry Project No. 2:
# What is Self-Directed Learning?

In its broadest meaning, "self-directed learning" describes a process in which individuals take the initiative, with or without the help of others, in diagnosing their learning needs, formulating learning goals, identifying human and material resources for learning, choosing and implementing appropriate learning strategies, and evaluating learning outcomes. Other labels found in the literature to describe this process are "self-planned learning," "inquiry method," "independent learning," "self-education," "self-instruction," "self-teaching," "self-study," and "autonomous learning." The trouble with most of these labels is that they seem to imply learning in isolation, whereas self-directed learning usually takes place in association with various kinds of helpers, such as teachers, tutors, mentors, resource people, and peers. There is a lot of mutuality among a group of self-directed learners.

## TWO APPROACHES TO EDUCATION

Perhaps the full meaning of self-directed learning can be made clearer by comparing it with its opposite, which was referred to in Inquiry Project No. 1 as being "taught." To make the labels parallel, let's call it "teacher-directed learning."

It might be worthwhile to mention in passing that the body of theory and practice on which teacher-directed learning is based is often given the label "pedagogy," from the Greek words *paid* (meaning "child") and *agogus* (meaning "leader"). Pedagogy has come to be defined as the art and science of teaching, but its tradition is in the teaching of children. The body of theory and practice on which self-directed learning is based has come to be labeled "andragogy," from the combining form *andr* of the Greek word *aner* (meaning "man"). Andragogy is defined, therefore, as the art and science of helping adults (or, even better, maturing human beings) learn. These definitions do not imply that children should be taught pedagogically and adults should be taught andragogically. Rather, the two terms simply differentiate between two sets of assumptions about learners, and the teacher who makes one set of assumptions will teach pedagogically whether he or she is teaching children or adults, whereas the teacher who makes the other set of assumptions will teach andragogically whether the learners are children or adults. In fact, many of the current innovations in schooling, such as open classrooms, nongraded schools, learning laboratories, community schools, and nontraditional study programs, are premised on andragogical assumptions about children and youth as learners.

The assumptions about learners on which these two approaches are based are summarized in Learning Resource A. You might find it helpful to scan it quickly now, and then turn back here and read the paragraphs below for any further explanation you may want.

Teacher-directed learning assumes the learner is essentially a dependent personality and that the teacher has the responsibility of deciding what and how the learner should be taught; whereas self-directed learning assumes that the human being grows in capacity (and need) to be self-directing as an essential component of maturing, and that this capacity should be nurtured to develop as rapidly as possible.

Teacher-directed learning assumes that the learner's experience is of less value than that of the teacher, the textbook writers and materials producers as a resource for learning, and that therefore the teacher has the responsibility to see to it that the resources of these experts are transmitted to the learner; whereas self-directed learning assumes that the learner's experiences become an increasingly rich resource for learning which should be exploited along with the resources of experts.

Teacher-directed learning assumes that students become ready to learn different things at different levels of maturation, and that a given set of learners will therefore be ready to learn the same things at a given level of maturation; whereas self-directed learning assumes that individuals become ready to learn what is required to perform their evolving life tasks or to cope more adequately with their life problems, and that each individual therefore has a somewhat different pattern of readiness from other individuals.

Teacher-directed learning assumes that students enter into education with a subject-centered orientation to learning (they see learning as accumulating subject matter) and that therefore learning experiences should be organized according to units of content; whereas self-directed learning assumes that this orientation is a result of their previous conditioning in school and that their natural orientation is task- or problem-centered, and that therefore learning experiences should be organized as task-accomplishing or problem-solving learning projects (or inquiry units).

Teacher-directed learning assumes that students are motivated to learn in response to external rewards and punishments, such as grades, diplomas, awards, degrees, and fear of failure; whereas self-directed learning assumes that learners are motivated by internal incentives, such as the need for esteem (especially self-esteem), the desire to achieve, the urge to grow, the satisfaction of accomplishment, the need to know something specific, and curiosity.

As you reflect on these differing assumptions, does it occur to you that both sets of assumptions may be true—that all teacher-directed learning is not necessarily bad and that all self-directed learning is not necessarily good? No doubt there are learning situations in which we are indeed dependent (as when approaching an entirely new and strange area of inquiry), in which our experience is in fact of little worth (as when we have had no previous experience within the area of inquiry), in which our readiness to learn is really determined by our level of maturation regarding the area of inquiry, in which we are rightly focusing on accumulating subject matter, and in which we are actually motivated by external pressures. Perhaps what makes the difference between pedagogical and andragogical education is not so much the difference in the assumptions underlying their theory and practice as it is the attitude of the learners. If self-directed learners recognize that there are occasions on which they will need to be taught, they will enter into those taught-learning situations in a searching, probing frame of mind and will exploit them as resources for learning without losing their self-directedness.

## RESOURCES FOR ADDITIONAL INQUIRY

Dressel, Paul L., and Mary M. Thompson. *Independent Study*. San Francisco: Jossey-Bass, 1973.

Gleason, Gerald T., ed. *The Theory and Nature of Independent Learning: A Symposium*. Scranton, Pa.: International Textbook Co., 1967.

Houle, Cyril O. *Continuing Your Education*. New York: McGraw-Hill, 1964.

————. *The Inquiring Mind*. Madison: University of Wisconsin Press, 1961.

Massialas, B. G., and J. Zevin. *Creative Encounters in the Classroom: Teaching and Learning Through Discovery*. New York: Wiley, 1967.

Silberman, M. L., J. S. Allender, and J. M. Yanoff. *The Psychology of Open Teaching and Learning: An Inquiry Approach*. Boston: Little, Brown, 1972.

Shulman, L. S., and E. R. Keislar. *Learning by Discovery: A Critical Appraisal*. Chicago: Rand McNally, 1966.

Tough, Allen. *Learning Without a Teacher*. Toronto: Ontario Institute for Studies in Education, 1967.

# Inquiry Project No. 3: What Competencies Are Required for Self-Directed Learning?

The competencies required to excel in teacher-directed learning, every *A*-student will tell you, include the ability to listen attentively, the ability to take careful notes, the ability to read speedily and with good comprehension, and the ability to predict exam questions and cram for them. This may seem to be a caricature of teacher-directed learning competencies, but aren't these in reality the ones we have come to rely upon in school?

Self-directed learning, however, requires a very different set of competencies. A list of the more general and important competencies are contained in Learning Resource B.

You might find it useful to turn to Learning Resource B now and rate the degree to which you already possess each of these competencies. Then check out your ratings with a group of two or three peers and a teacher to get their help in testing how realistic your ratings are.

## *RESOURCES FOR ADDITIONAL INQUIRY*

The resources listed at the end of Inquiry Project No. 2 have some information about the competencies required for self-directed learning. But the following resource provides the most detailed description of required competencies:

Tough, Allen. *The Adult's Learning Projects*. Toronto: Ontario Institute for Studies in Education, 1971, chapters 6, 7, 9, 10.

# Inquiry Project No. 4: Designing a Learning Plan

There are a variety of ways one can go about designing a plan for learning. Perhaps the simplest is to follow the steps of scientific inquiry:

1. What is the question I want an answer to?
2. What are the data I need to answer this question?
3. What are the most appropriate and feasible sources of these data?
4. What are the most efficient and effective means I can use to collect these data from these sources?
5. How shall I organize and analyze these data to get an answer to my question?
6. How will I report my answer and test its validity?

But I want to suggest a somewhat more elaborate and rigorous format: a *learning contract*. My students report that it helps them organize their learning more efficiently, induces them to be more creative in identifying learning resources and developing learning strategies, and forces them to get better evidence of their accomplishments. It is capable of being used in any content area.

## THE LEARNING CONTRACT

A contract is usually defined as "a binding agreement between two or more persons or parties," and it is in fact becoming more and more common for teachers to make contracts with students for course work and grades, and for nontraditional study institutions to enter into contracts with students specifying what must be accomplished to earn a particular degree. For the purpose of this learning project in self-directed learning, however, I suggest that you contract with yourself. You are contracting with yourself to become a self-directed learner, and your contract will specify how you will go about it and how you will know when you are there.

Here are some suggestions for building your learning contract:

1. Turn to Learning Resource C and reproduce on three or four sheets of typing paper the four-column form of the contract (1. Learning Objectives; 2. Learning Resources and Strategies; 3. Evidence of Accomplishment; and 4. Criteria and Means of Validating).

2. Scan down Column 1 of the sample contract in Learning Resource C and, on the basis of the assessment you made in Inquiry Project No. 3, write into Column 1 of your contract form any objectives that you feel it would be useful for you to work toward. Add any other objectives not in this list that you can think of on your own.

3. Go now to Column 2 of your contract form and for each learning objective identify one or more learning resources and strategies that you think will help you accomplish that objective. Learning Resources J and K describe some learning strategies that are relevant to various kinds of objectives; you may well think of others.

4. Now you are ready for Column 3, in which for each objective you specify what evidence you will collect to help you measure the degree to which you have accomplished that objective. Learning Resource C and Learning Resource N will give you some ideas about what kinds of evidence are appropriate for different objectives. You, in turn, may think of other kinds of evidence that will have meaning for you.

5. Column 4 provides space for you to indicate what criteria you will use for judging the evidence, and what means you will use to convince yourself of the validity of the evidence. Learning Resource O may suggest ideas for this step. This is probably the most difficult part of the whole process, so don't try to be too ambitious about being scientific. The important thing is that you have some experience in weighing the evidence about what you have learned and judging how convincing it is to *you*.

6. At this point, you will find it helpful to check out your learning contract with a teacher or a group of peers. You can ask them such questions as:

    a. Are the learning objectives clear, understandable, and realistic?

    b. Can they think of other objectives you might consider?

    c. Do the learning strategies seem reasonable?

    d. Can they think of other resources and strategies you might consider?

    e. Does the evidence seem relevant to the various objectives?

    f. Can they suggest other evidence you might consider?

    g. Are the criteria and means for validating the evidence clear, relevant, and convincing?

      **h.** Can they think of other ways to validate the evidence you might consider?

7. From the responses you get from the above consultants, you may wish to modify your contract.

Now you are ready to engage in the learning strategies specified in your contract.

*Have a rewarding experience.*

# PART II
# THE TEACHER

---

# For the Teacher

Welcome to an adventure in turning students on to learning. I'd like to start off with you, as I did with the learners, by setting a climate for our mutual inquiry. So I suggest that if you haven't already read what I said to the learners in Part I, you turn there now and scan it. I'd like for the same social climate to exist in our relationship that I set up for them: warm, mutually respectful, dialogic, and mutually trustful.

### Setting a Climate

The nature of the inquiry you and I will be engaging in is somewhat different from the inquiry the learners and I engaged in. The objective of my inquiry with them was to help them learn to become self-directed learners. The nature of my inquiry with you will be to explore the implications for teachers of having self-directed learners as students. The broad question we shall inquire into is this: "What should be my role, what competencies will I need, and what strategies should I use if I am to teach self-directed learners?"

In order to minimize any temptation on my part to take a didactic cook-book stance, let me open up the inquiry by presenting myself as a case study.

# Defining a New Role

## From Content Transmitter . . .

When I first started experimenting at encouraging students to be self-directed learners, I experienced a severe dissonance in the conception of my own role. I had been trained to perceive my role as essentially that of content-transmitter and judge of the students' absorption of the transmitted content. Accordingly, in performing this role, I saw my main function as preparing and executing a content plan, which involved my answering only the following four questions:

1. *What content needs to be covered?*
   So I would list all the concepts, principles, facts, and skills that should be covered in a given course. I might add that my conditioning had been such that I thought in terms of what should be *covered*, not what should be *learned*.

2. *How can this content be organized into manageable units?*
   So I would arrange the content into one-hour units, three-hour units, one-semester units, or whatever other size of units the schedule required.

31

3. *How can these units be organized into a logical sequence?*

So I would try to figure out the inherent logic of whatever subject matter content I was teaching. If it was historical information, the sequence from ancient to modern seemed obvious—although I later learned that the way we actually gain historical perspective is the reverse of that. If it was skill-development content, movement from simple to complex skills was the sequence of choice—even though, if I had thought about it, I would have remembered that I learned to swim by learning the more complex skill of staying afloat first and then later learned the simpler skill of flutter-kicking.

4. *What means of transmission will be most efficient for transmitting each unit?*

So I would decide which unit would be transmitted by lecture, which by assigned reading, which by audio-visual presentation, and so forth.

Then, of course, I would have to administer tests to find out how much of the content the students had received and absorbed. And when the test results were less than satisfactory, I naturally assumed that the fault lay with the students' reception, and not with my transmission.

I must admit, in retrospect, that I think I was a pretty good transmitter. My content was well organized, with a good logical outline; I illustrated abstract concepts or principles with interesting examples; I spoke clearly and dynamically; I brought forth frequent chuckles with my humor; I invited interruptions for questions of clarification at any time; and I had lively discussions and practice exercises following my lectures when there was time. I think my tests were quite fair, too—always producing a pretty good curve of distribution.

When I started encouraging students to be self-directed learners, I initially assumed that they would change but I would perform the same. The only difference would be that they would take more responsibility for making use of my transmissions, planning their outside reading, and producing more creative term papers. I had a couple of early shocks as a result of this assumption. The first was when I discovered that my students didn't want to be self-directed learners; they wanted me to teach them. Then, when I got them over that hurdle—through strategies I shall describe shortly—they really got turned on about being self-directed learners and forced me to change my role.

Rather than bore you with the long process this transition involved, let me describe how I see my role as it has evolved up to this point (and I hope it will continue to evolve as my students help me to learn how to do it better).

### ... To Facilitator of Learning

In the first place, my self-concept has changed from that of teacher to that of facilitator of learning. This may seem to be a simple and perhaps even superficial change. But I found it to be fundamental and terribly difficult. It required that I focus on what was happening in the students rather than on what I was doing. It required that I divest myself of the protective shield of an authority figure and expose myself as *me*—an authentic human being, with feelings, hopes, aspirations, insecurities, worries, strengths, and weaknesses. It required that I be clear about precisely what resources I did and did not have that might be useful to the learners, and that I make the resources I did have accessible to them on their terms. It required that I extricate myself from the compulsion to pose as an expert who had mastered any given body of content and, instead, join my students honestly as a continuing co-learner.

In the second place, I have found myself performing quite a different set of functions from those involved in transmitting (although I still do some transmitting when the self-directed learners ask for it), and that therefore I have had to develop a different set of skills. I found myself, for example, functioning primarily as a procedural guide and only secondarily as a resource for content information. To clarify the concept "procedural guide," let me compare the questions I now ask in preparing an educational program with the questions I listed earlier that I asked when I thought of myself as a content transmitter. I ask myself, "What procedures shall I use (or present to the learners as options) that are likely to be most effective with this particular group of learners, in this particular setting, given this particular area of inquiry, for accomplishing the following seven elements of an andragogical process design?"

1. *Climate setting.*

   How can I most quickly get the learners to become acquainted with one another as persons and as mutual resources for learning? How can I help them to gain an understanding of the concept of self-directed learning? How can I provide them with a simple preliminary experience in practising the skills of self-directed learning? How can I help them to understand my role as a facilitator and resource to self-directed learners and ensure that they will feel comfortable in relating to me this way? How can I present myself to them as a human being so that they may trust me? How can I provide them with a short but meaningful experience in working together collaboratively? How can I create an atmosphere characterized by both mutual caring and support and intellectual rigor?

**2.** *Planning.*

At what points shall I decide what procedures to use, and at what points shall I present optional procedures for them to decide about? On what ethical basis shall I make this decision, and how will I explain it to them and invite their modification or veto? What mechanism will I propose for involving them in the decision-making process—consensus or voting by the total group, delegation of responsibility to subgroups, or delegation to an elected steering committee?

**3.** *Diagnosing needs for learning.*

How shall we construct a model of the competencies (or content objectives, if you prefer) this particular learning experience should be concerned with? If I start with a model I have constructed, how can I present it so that they will feel free to change it or build upon it? If I start with their suggestions for a model, how can I introduce my own ideas or the requirements from the outer environment without denigrating their contributions? How can I assure that they will have a sense of ownership of the model finally agreed upon? How can I make it possible for them realistically and nonthreateningly to assess the gaps between their present level of development of the competencies and the level required by the model?

4. *Setting goals.*

How can I help them translate diagnosed needs into learning objectives that are clear, feasible, at appropriate levels of specificity or generality, personally meaningful, and measurable as to accomplishment? How can I suggest changes constructively?

5. *Designing a learning plan.*

What guidelines for designing a learning plan will I propose? What optional models of plans will I present? What kinds of help will I give particular learners in designing their plans? How will I expose them to resources and strategies for using resources that they may not know about or may not have thought of? What mechanisms (*e.g.*, consultation teams) can I suggest to facilitate their helping one another in designing their plans?

6. *Engaging in learning activities.*

Which learning activities shall I take responsibility for to meet objectives that are common to all (or most) of their learning plans, which activities should be the responsibility of subgroups, and which should be individual inquiry projects? How can I make myself available to subgroups and individuals as a consultant and resource as they plan and carry out their learning activities? What is my responsibility for assuring quality performance of the learning activities?

7. *Evaluating learning outcomes.*

What should be my role in feeding data to the learners regarding my perceptions of the accomplishment of their learning objectives? How can I do it so as not to create a dissonance with the learners' self-directedness? What is my responsibility for making judgments about the adequacy of the evidence of accomplishment of the learners' objectives and the adequacy of their criteria and means for validating their evidence? How can I present these judgments in such a way that they will enhance rather than diminish the learners' self-concepts as self-directed persons?

I have encountered several conceptual problems in presenting this new role to learners that it is probably appropriate to discuss now, before getting into some of the more technical problems in the next section.

One problem concerns the issue of structure versus nonstructure. Many students enter into a new learning situation feeling a deep need for the security of a clear structural plan—an outline, course syllabus, time schedule, and the like. They want teachers who know what they are doing, who are in charge. When they first hear me describe my perception of the role of a facilitator and resource to self-directed learners it seems so structureless to them that they become anxious. So I have learned to emphasize that we shall be working within a structure, but that it is a different kind of structure from what they have been used to—that it is a process structure; whereas they have been used to a content structure. And I assure them that I am in charge of the process, that I shall make decisions about procedures when they aren't in a position to make them with me, and that I know what I am doing. I assure them that I understand that they are being asked to take more responsibility for learning than they are used to, and that I shall help them learn to do it.

This raises a second problem, which concerns the issue of "content" versus "no content." Students want to be sure that they are going to get the required content to pass their exams, get certified, obtain licenses, get accepted into other institutions, or get jobs. I deal with this problem head-on by explaining that the difference between a content-transmission plan and a process design is not that one deals with content and the other does not, but that one is concerned with the transmission of content and the other with the acquisition of content. I refer them to the chart in Learning Resource A and point out that as a result of going through the first four phases of the process design on the right half of the chart (climate setting, planning, diagnosing needs, and setting goals) we arrive at a clear definition of the content they are to acquire.

A third problem, which arises only in institutional settings in which grades are required, is how the grades will be arrived at fairly. I deal with this problem by inviting the students to draft contracts in which they specify on separate sheets what objectives they propose fulfilling for a *C*, a *B*, and an *A*. I study these first drafts very carefully and frequently write my detailed reactions indicating what revisions will have to be made in the contracts in order for me to find them acceptable at the levels of grade specified. Only when a contract is revised to the point where it calls for a level of performance that I feel represents *A* quality will I agree to a contract for an *A*. I must confess that this system puts a lot of pressure on students in a competitive academic environment to overextend themselves, and I frequently find myself encouraging students to contract for a *B* or *C* rather than to sacrifice their health or possible achievement in other courses. On the other hand, it has been my experience that this system produces a high degree of motivation along with an output of energy that results in superior learning.

# Developing Self-Directed
# Learners

As I see it, the first responsibility of a facilitator of learning is to help students develop competence as self-directed
learners. I can visualize four optional strategies you might
use for doing this:

1. You could ask the students individually (preferably,
I should think, before classes start) to turn to Part I of
this book and engage in Inquiry Projects 1, 2, 3, and 4 on
their own—coming to you only when they want help.
Then, at the opening session of the first class you have
with them, you could have them analyze their experience
and raise unresolved issues or unanswered questions.

2. You could team the students up into small groups
of from two to five and ask them to pursue the Inquiry
Projects independently as teams—coming to you only
when they need help, and also having them analyze their
experience in the first session of class.

3. You could involve all of a given group of students
(for instance, all the entering freshmen, or all the students
in a given department, or all the students for whom you
are the adviser, or all the students you will have in your
courses) in an intensive two-day workshop on self-directed

learning. One model of a design for such a workshop, which is based on the assumption that all the students will have a copy of this book, is as follows:

    a. *Climate setting:*

        (1) Presentation of your perception of the purpose of this workshop and of your—and their—role in it.

        (2) Relationship-building exercise. (Learning Resource E.)

        (3) Why self-directed learning? (Inquiry Project 1, followed by discussion of agreements, disagreements, questions, and suggestions for further inquiry.)

        (4) What is self-directed learning? (Inquiry Project 2, followed by a discussion of the assumptions and process elements presented in Learning Resource A.)

    b. *Diagnosis of needs for learning (about self-directed learning):*

        (1) What competencies are required? (Inquiry Project 3.)

        (2) Rating by each student of his or her present level of competencies. (Learning Resource B, with students sharing their self-ratings in consultation groups of from three to five.)

    c. *Designing a learning plan* (Inquiry Project 4):

        (1) Have each student make out a first draft of a learning contract, using the model in Learning Resource C.

        (2) Have each student present his or her contract to the above consultation group of peers and get their suggestions for improvement.

    (3) Collect the revised contracts and, while the students have free time, add your own suggestions to each contract.

    (4) Return the contracts to the students and give them time to make revisions in the light of your suggestions.

  d. *Conducting learning activities:*

    (1) The students could be given the choice of working on the learning strategies specified in their contracts either individually or in self-selected inquiry groups.

    (2) Your role would be to be available as a consultant and resource person as specified in the Inquiry Projects or Learning Resources.

  e. *Evaluating learning outcomes:*

    (1) Have each student present the evidence specified in his or her contract to the consultation group constituted above in *b*.

    (2) Invite a sample of students to share their contracts and evidences with the total group, with you reacting and drawing generalizations.

    (3) Have the students form new groups of five or six each and evaluate the total experience, with feedback to you by a designated spokesman for each group.

4. If copies of this book will not be available to all the students, you could provide them with at least an introductory orientation to the concept and skills of self-directed learning through the following three-hour design which I developed for our entering degree candidates:

All new students are invited to attend a three-hour orientation session during the week before classes start or, if this isn't feasible, the opening week of the term, with a choice among two or three time periods. Each student is asked to bring an information-resource book (not a novel or creative essay), preferably with its dust jacket still on it, and with a table of contents and index. The students sit in groups of five or six, around tables or in circles of chairs, as they enter the room.

In opening the session, I (or perhaps I may call on a veteran student to do this) explain that they are entering a program in which they will be expected to take a good deal of responsibility and initiative in their learning, and that the purpose of this orientation session is to acquaint them with the concept and to give them some skill practice in self-directed learning. I then explain that the design for the session consists of four activities: (a) development of a cognitive map; (b) a relationship-building exercise; (c) a proactive reading exercise, and (d) an exercise in utilization of peer resources. These activities are conducted as follows:

    a. *Development of a cognitive map:*

        (1) Pass out reproductions of the chart, "A Comparison of Assumptions and Processes of Transmitted Learning and Self-Directed Learning" which is displayed in Learning Resource A.

        (2) Ask the students to examine the left half of the chart ("Assumptions") and raise any questions that will tend to help them understand what it means. (I will respond only after inviting other students to respond first.)

        (3) Then ask the students to examine the right half of the chart ("Process Elements") and similarly raise questions for clarification.

(4) Pass out reproductions of the chart, "Competencies of Self-directed Learning," displayed in Learning Resource B, and invite the students to raise questions of clarification, and then to rate themselves. (I have found that students find it supportive if they share their self-ratings in their small groups.)

b. *Relationship-building exercise* (Learning Resource E).

c. *Using material resources proactively* (Learning Resource L).

d. *Using human resources proactively* (Learning Resource M).

e. *Analyzing this experience:*

(1) Engage the students in learning through the analysis of their experience by asking such questions as:

(a) How differently do you feel about your fellow students from the way you usually do in a class?

(b) How do you feel about being a self-directed learner?

(c) In what regards do you feel need for help in becoming more self-directed as a learner, and how will you go about getting this help?

# Implementing the Role of Facilitator

I am now going to undertake a very risky venture. I am going to describe how I go about performing as a facilitator and resource to self-directed learners in a content-oriented course.

One risk is that the content of the course I am going to be using for illustration will be so different from the content of the courses you teach that you may be tempted to write off the illustration as irrelevant to your situation. This it may be, but, on the other hand, I have used this same approach in a number of content areas having to do with professional development, and my students have used it in courses ranging from liberal arts to highly technical subjects, with a variety of adaptations, and it has almost universally seemed to produce more enthusiastic and accomplished learners.

Another risk is that the description of what I do may be interpreted as the right way—or best way—to do it. But I am going to describe my performance in a very narrow, specialized content area: a graduate course in "The Nature of Adult Education." I would perform the role differently in different content areas in which I was more or less an expert resource and in which other resources were more or less available. Furthermore, different people performing the role in precisely the same situations would perform it differently, adapting it to their individual personalities, styles, and resources. So we are talking about a basic process that can be implemented in a variety of ways. I shall be describing only my way, at this particular stage of my development. Note that I am willing to take these risks if you are willing to let me be me.

I have offered the course, "EO700: The Nature of Adult Education," for fifteen years, with enrollments ranging from thirty to sixty students. The basic content objectives and process elements have been constant, but each year I have experimented with differed procedures, so the course has not been the same twice. The course would meet one afternoon a week, from four o'clock to seven o'clock, for fifteen weeks. Usually the course was assigned a room with movable chairs that could easily be arranged five or six chairs to a circle; on a few occasions we had a room with small tables and five or six chairs to a table, which I prefer.

Here is how I have tried to be a facilitator and resource to self-directed learners in this course:

1. FIRST MEETING.
   (Orientation, climate setting, and relationship building.)

As students enter the room I welcome them and introduce myself. I give each student a 5-by-8-inch plain card and a felt pen and ask them to fold the card and write his or her name on it, and then place it on the arm of the chair or on the table so that everybody can see it.

When it appears that most of the students have arrived,

I introduce myself again and explain that in this course I am making certain assumptions about learning and about mature learners that they should be aware of and have a chance to react to. I then distribute the chart, "A Comparison of Assumptions and Processes of Teacher-directed Learning and Self-Directed Learning" (Learning Resource A). I ask them first to scan the left side and raise any questions about the assumptions, and then I ask them to scan the right side and raise any questions they have about the processes. This dialogue may go on for fifteen to thirty minutes, during which time I take the opportunity to elaborate on my perception of my role as a facilitator and resource and their role as self-directed learners.

I next explain that as they look at one another in this classroom, they see one another as competitors because this has been their conditioning from previous schooling, but that the approach we are using in this course requires that they relate to one another as mutual helpers. This is the rationale for taking a few minutes to engage in the relationship-building exercise described in Learning Resource E.

I then pass out the course syllabus, which contains the following elements:

a. *Course objectives.*
   I explain that these objectives describe the competencies of knowledge, understanding, skill, attitude, and value that my own experience and some research seem to indicate are possessed by excellent practitioners in the field of adult education that are within the scope of this course, but that the students should read them critically and be prepared at the next session to suggest modifications.

b. *Resources for learning.*

I review the bibliographical references, pointing out the kind of information contained in each one, and suggest some of the human resources available among the members of the class, among the faculty of the university (including myself), and in the community.

c. *Units of inquiry.*

This section of the syllabus proposes the areas of inquiry (Learning Resource H) that are appropriate to this course, and identifies some of the material and human resources that are especially relevant to each unit. I review these units, elaborating on their meaning, and suggesting why it is useful for adult educators to have competence in these areas. I invite the students, as this review is being done, to suggest other areas they would like to inquire into.

I then pass out reproductions of Learning Resource H and suggest that during the following week the students scan the resources mentioned in the syllabus and start listing on the right side of Learning Resource H the areas they feel the need to inquire into further.

I close the first session by inviting questions on any areas that haven't been dealt with adequately. The question most frequently asked at this point is how the grade will be arrived at. To this I suggest that they be thinking about what they would like to propose in this regard for us to discuss at the next session.

2. SECOND MEETING.

(Diagnosis of needs for learning and formulating objectives.)

I open the second session by reviewing what happened

at the first session and inviting any new students to introduce themselves.

I then explain that during the remainder of the course
the students are going to be using one another frequently
as consultants, and that therefore it might be useful for
them to have some practice in using skills of consultation.
I describe an exercise designed for this purpose, and ask
for a show of hands as to who would like to do it; so far,
the majority of students have raised their hands, but if they
hadn't, we would have skipped the exercise (also, I always
leave the option open for those who don't want to do it to
spend the time at something else). So the students spon-
taneously form triads and we do the exercise described
in Learning Resource F, with the problem each student
presents to his or her consultant being the adequacy of his
self-diagnosis of learning needs as developed in his use
of Learning Resource H.

This exercise takes one hour. Following it, I call the
class to order and ask if other areas of inquiry have sur-
faced that are not included in the syllabus. In almost every
class one or two other areas are suggested, and these are
added to the syllabus and to Learning Resource H.

I then suggest that it probably would be useful for us
to get an over-all picture of the distribution of learning
needs among the members of the class. The most efficient
technique I have found for accomplishing this task is to
put the students back into groups of five or six, with each
group pooling the needs of its members into a frequency
distribution, and then building a master frequency distribution on the chalk board from the composite reports of
all the groups. This process enables each student to identify what other students are interested in the same areas
of inquiry, and it provides me with an opportunity to
"make a case" for some areas that seem to be neglected.

Next, I explain that the task for the next week is to construct first drafts of learning contracts. I pass out copies of contract forms containing only the headings of the form illustrated in Learning Resource C, along with two or three examples of completed contracts selected from previous students who have taken this course and the "Guidelines for Contract Learning" reproduced in the Appendix. I invite and respond to questions about how to fill out each of the four columns in the contract. I explain that a student may contract for a *C*, a *B*, or an *A*, but that students contracting for one of the higher grades must indicate on separate sheets what parts of their contracts are for the lower grades. (Thus, a student contracting for an *A* would have one sheet indicating his *A*-level contract, another sheet indicating his *B*-level contract, and a third sheet showing his *C*-level contract). I have found from experience that this system helps students to think through what differentiates an excellent level of performance from adequate and passing levels.

I explain that I will collect the first drafts of these contracts at the next session of the class and will return them, along with my comments and suggestions, at the beginning of the fourth meeting. I also suggest that during the week the class be thinking about which unit of inquiry, if any, they would like to probe into deeply as a member of an inquiry team.

3. THIRD MEETING.
(Designing learning plans.)

As soon as all students have arrived I ask them to get into the triads they formed the previous week in doing the consultation skill practice exercise. I explain that these triads will be available for consultation at any time one member wants help during the remainder of the semester.

I point out that the task now is to test the adequacy of the learning contracts that have been drafted during the week, and I suggest that this be done by each student taking twenty minutes to present his or her contract and getting feedback from the other two members of the triad. I suggest that the consultants might raise these questions about each contract:

   a. Concerning the objectives:
      (1) Are they clear and understandable?
      (2) Do they really describe what the individual is undertaking to learn (rather than what he or she plans to do)?
      (3) Are they stated in such a way that the degree to which they are accomplished can be estimated or measured?
      (4) Is the differentiation between *C*-level, *B*-level, and *A*-level objectives reasonable?
   b. Concerning the learning strategies:
      (1) Are the resources proposed for each objective the most authoritative, reliable, and feasible available?
      (2) Are there other resources—especially human resources—that should be considered?
      (3) Are the methods and techniques proposed for making use of the resources the most effective possible?
   c. Concerning the evidence of accomplishment of objectives:
      (1) Is the evidence proposed for each objective clearly relevant to that objective?
      (2) Is it the best evidence possible; will it be convincing to the consultants?
      (3) Can the consultants suggest other kinds of evidence that might be considered?

    d. Concerning the criteria and means for validating the evidence:

        (1) Are the criteria proposed for judging the evidence of accomplishment of each objective clear, relevant, and able to be applied?

        (2) Should other criteria be considered?

        (3) Do the means proposed for judging the evidence by these criteria seem appropriate, feasible, and convincing?

        (4) Should other means be considered?

(Incidentally, I might point out that these are the questions I raise when I am consulting with individual students in independent study or degree contracting.)

After the triads have completed reviewing the contracts of all three members, I suggest that the students take another twenty to thirty minutes to revise their contracts in the light of the feedback they have received, and then I collect the contracts.

Our next task, I suggest, is for us to organize the resources of the class for conducting the inquiry into those units that all or most students have included in their contracts (leaving to individual students responsibility for pursuing the objectives that are more personal and individualistic). We accomplish this task by reviewing the inquiry units in the syllabus (which are also those reproduced in Learning Resource H) and agreeing (as a total group) on the answers to these questions regarding each unit:

1. Should it be included in the plan for the total class or should it be left for those individuals who have it in their contracts to pursue? If the former, then:

        a. Should an inquiry team of students take responsibility for it?

        b. Should I take responsibility for it?

c. Should we bring in an outside resource to handle it?

Typically this procedure has resulted in six to eight units being delegated to inquiry teams and one or two to me or to an outside resource. The next step, therefore, is to organize inquiry teams. I do this by asking each student to make a first, second, and third choice of the units he or she would like to participate in, based on the priority order of his or her needs and interests. Then, by a show of hands, we find out how many students select each unit as their first choice. If more than eight students select one unit, negotiations are entered into to try to get students with strong second choices to move over to a smaller team. (It has been my experience that when teams are larger than eight they have difficulty organizing for work.)

The option is left open for students to elect to work on individual projects rather than to participate in an inquiry team, and usually in a class of thirty about half a dozen will elect to do so. But frequently these "independents" organize themselves into mutual-help groups to share their experiences in their independent projects.

Usually there is sufficient time left in this third session for the inquiry teams to have a brief meeting to get acquainted, identify special interests, and agree on tasks to be pursued in the following week. Before the teams meet, however, I review the responsibilities they have undertaken and suggest possible ways to organize to carry out their responsibilities. For example, in this course the task of each team is to learn all it can from the literature and from resource people on campus and in the community about its content unit and then to plan how it can present a learning experience to the rest of the class to help them get the essence of what the team learned about its unit. The tasks of all teams are reviewed in open meeting, so that all teams understand the tasks of the other teams and so that problems of territorial conflict can be resolved. I strongly urge the members of the teams to take time in their first meeting to build relationships with one another as persons before starting to work.

4. FOURTH MEETING.
  (Contract revision and team planning.)

During the week between the third and fourth meetings I block off ample time in my date book to allow me to study the contracts carefully and to write my questions, reactions, and suggestions either in the margins or on separate slips of paper which are then clipped to the contracts. As students enter the room at the beginning of the fourth session I hand them their contracts and allow about half an hour for them to examine my comments and consult with me about them. Then I suggest that those students who want to revise their contracts do so in the following week and turn the revised versions in to me at the fifth session. I emphasize that the contracts are subject to renegotiation at any time through the twelfth session, on the score that their objectives, strategies, and ideas about evidence may change as a result of their inquiry experiences.

The remaining time (usually over two hours) of this session is devoted to team meetings, while I stand by for consultation or resource help. During this first meeting of the teams, the members usually probe one another's interests and resources more deeply than was possible in the large meetings, review their resource materials, and then divide responsibility among themselves for carrying out their inquiry. Frequently a coordinator is elected at this session, although many teams are able to operate efficiently without designated leadership.

5. FIFTH, SIXTH, AND SEVENTH MEETINGS.
   (Team work.)

At the beginning of the fifth session I receive any revised contracts, which I agree to return the following
week. At the start of each of these three sessions I also
ask if any team has run into problems that need the attention of all of us, and I emphasize that I am available
during these sessions as a consultant and resource person.
(In my early experience with inquiry teams I discovered
that there was a reluctance to use me as a helper, probably
because that might be interpreted as a sign of dependence.
So, in recent years, I have made a point of raising this as
an issue before the teams start working, and suggesting
that one of the competencies of self-directed learning is
the ability to make effective use of human as well as material resources. I even take the time often to spell out the
resources I have that might be useful to the teams.)

At the beginning of the seventh meeting I point out that
the task now facing the teams is to design learning experiences which will enable the rest of the students to acquire
the content of their respective inquiry units. I urge them
to consider carefully how they can design experiences that
will involve the other students actively in an inquiry, rather
than settle for a design in which the content will be transmitted to them as passive recipients. I usually give illustrations of both types of design from previous classes, and
suggest resources (such as my *Modern Practice of Adult
Education*) that might help them with ideas about the designing of learning experiences. At this point, also, we
agree on dates for the teams' presentations, and I remind
them that the evidence of fulfillment of their contracts is
due at the thirteenth meeting. (I should point out that it
is quite common for a team to require more time to com-

plete the design of its learning experience, and so out-of-class team meetings are often arranged.)

A part of the scheduling of dates for team presentations is agreement as to the amount of time each team will have. Some inquiry units are more complex than others and require more time. Typically about half the teams accept a one-hour limitation, with the understanding that I shall have a half hour following the presentation to introduce additional or corrective information and to engage the entire class in an analysis of the team's design. On about half the dates, therefore, two teams make their presentations. The other half of the teams are allocated a two-hour period, with me having one hour for comment and analysis. I might add that my input at these sessions is often quite substantial, but the fact that it is building on what the students have contributed causes it to be received less as a transmission than as a continuation of dialogue.

6. EIGHTH THROUGH THIRTEENTH MEETINGS.
   (Presentation of learning experiences.)

In the early years of my experimentation with inquiry teams, several of the team presentations tended to be fairly stereotypic transmissions of information by lectures, audio-visual presentations, panel discussions, symposiums, and the like. The norm seemed to become established that every team member must have equal time "on the air." But as students gained more experience and got feedback on their presentations, this norm gave way to the norm that presentations should be creative and involving, regardless of how many students on the team got to show off. By now, most team presentations are highly creative experiments in participative learning, with such designs as micro-workshops, simulated field experiences, participative cases, telelectures, group interviews of experts, original dramatic presentations, and the like. Almost all teams prepare handout materials, ranging from annotated bibliographies to elaborate collections of reprints, manuals, guidelines, and instruments.

At the end of the twelfth session I remind the students that their contracts, with supportive evidence of fulfillment, are due at the beginning of the next meeting.

### 7. FOURTEENTH MEETING.

(Completion of contract evidence.)

As soon as all the students have arrived I ask them to group themselves into the consultative triads that were formed in the second meeting. I suggest that each student be allotted up to forty-five minutes to present evidence of accomplishment of objectives to his or her two consultants; with them raising such questions as these:

    a. Concerning the evidence of accomplishment:

        (1) Is the evidence for each objective clearly relevant to that objective?

        (2) Is the evidence reliable and convincing?

    b. Concerning the criteria and means for validating the evidence:

        (1) Are the criteria clear and comprehensive?

        (2) Has the evidence been convincingly validated according to these criteria?

        (3) How would we rate the degree of accomplishment of each objective?

Frequently students use their consultants as validators of evidence they are in a position to judge, such as the student's contribution to the class. Examples of ratings scales students have constructed for this purpose are presented in Learning Resource O.

During the remaining time in the three-hour period I ask the triads to pool their thinking about any unresolved questions or issues concerning the content of the course that should be raised in the last meeting.

## 8. FIFTEENTH MEETING.
(Course evaluation.)

As the students enter the room I hand them back their contracts and portfolios of evidence, with my comments and proposed grade. Then I suggest that if they have any question about my comments or the grade they talk with me after class or in my office.

For the next hour I invite the students to raise unresolved questions or issues, to each of which I respond.

Then I announce that I need their evaluation of the entire course and my performance as a facilitator and resource. (I have experimented with a number of instruments and procedures for collecting evaluative data, but the one that seems to produce the best results is the simplest of all.) I form random groups of five or six students each—simply by having them count off and then designating different areas of the room for those with the various numbers to congregate. The charge to each group is twofold: They are *a*) to agree among themselves as to the three or four most useful evaluative questions that might be asked about a learning experience of this kind, and *b*) to tabulate the answers the members of the group give to these questions. I ask each group to select one person to report the tabulations.

I find that the groups usually complete their tasks in thirty to forty minutes, and then I call on the group reporters to read each question and the answers to it. My experience has been that the questions are usually very thoughtful and probing, and that the answers are highly positive. But I have yet to go through this process without getting at least one—and often several—suggestions for major improvement in the course procedures and my performance. I close the session by thanking the students for their help.

(If you are interested in seeing how I conducted an earlier version of this same course, without learning contracts, see pages 371–376 of my *Modern Practice of Adult Education: Andragogy versus Pedagogy.*)

I hope that you will have as exciting and rewarding a time as I have had in learning how to be a facilitator and resource to self-directed learners.

## RESOURCES FOR ADDITIONAL INQUIRY

Houle, Cyril O. *The Design of Education.* San Francisco: Jossey-Bass, 1972, pp. 31–58.

Knowles, Malcolm S. *The Modern Practice of Adult Education: Andragogy versus Pedagogy.* New York: Association Press, 1970, pp. 269–301.

Rogers, Carl R. *Freedom to Learn.* Columbus: Charles E. Merrill, 1969, pp. 57–97, 157–168.

Silberman, Melvin L., Jerome S. Allender, and Jay M. Yanoff. *The Psychology of Open Teaching and Learning.* Boston: Little, Brown, 1972, pp. 215–304.

Tough, Allen. *The Adult's Learning Projects.* Toronto: Ontario Institute for Studies in Education, 1971, pp. 147–166.

# PART III
# LEARNING RESOURCES

The following learning resources are designed to enhance the inquiry of both self-directed learners and facilitators of self-directed learning into the ideas and skills required for performing these respective roles.

Suggestions for using these resources are contained in Parts I and II.

# LEARNING RESOURCE A

## A COMPARISON OF ASSUMPTIONS AND PROCESSES OF TEACHER-DIRECTED (PEDAGOGICAL) LEARNING AND SELF-DIRECTED (ANDRAGOGICAL) LEARNING

(Please read as poles on a spectrum, not as black-and-white differences)

### ASSUMPTIONS

| About | Teacher-directed learning. | Self-directed learning |
|---|---|---|
| Concept of the learner | Dependent personality | Increasingly self-directed organism |
| Role of learner's experience | To be built on more than used | A rich resource for learning |
| Readiness to learn | Varies with levels of maturation | Develops from life tasks and problems |
| Orientation to learning | Subject-centered | Task- or problem-centered |
| Motivation | External rewards and punishments | Internal incentives, curiosity |

### PROCESS ELEMENTS

| Elements | Teacher-directed learning | Self-directed learning |
|---|---|---|
| Climate | Formal Authority-oriented Competitive Judgmental | Informal Mutually respectful Consensual Collaborative Supportive |
| Planning | Primarily by teacher | By participative decision-making |
| Diagnosis of needs | Primarily by teacher | By mutual assessment |
| Setting goals | Primarily by teacher | By mutual negotiation |
| Designing a learning plan | Content units Course syllabus Logical sequence | Learning projects Learning contracts Sequenced in terms of readiness |
| Learning activities | Transmittal techniques Assigned readings | Inquiry projects Independent study Experiential techniques |
| Evaluation | Primarily by teacher | By mutual assessment of self-collected evidence |

The body of theory and practice on which teacher-directed learning is based is often given the label "pedagogy," from the Greek words *paid* (meaning "child") and *agogus* (meaning "guide")--thus being defined as the art and science of teaching children.

The body of theory and practice on which self-directed learning is based is coming to be labeled "andragogy," from the Greek word *aner* (meaning "adult")--thus being defined as the art and science of helping adults (or even better, maturing human beings) learn.

# LEARNING RESOURCE B

**I possess these competencies to the following degree:**

## COMPETENCIES OF SELF-DIRECTED LEARNING: A SELF-RATING INSTRUMENT

| | None | Weak | Fair | Strong |
|---|---|---|---|---|
| 1. An understanding of the differences in assumptions about learners and the skills required for learning under teacher-directed learning and self-directed learning, and the ability to explain these differences to others. | | | | |
| 2. A concept of myself as being a non-dependent and a self-directing person. | | | | |
| 3. The ability to relate to peers collaboratively, to see them as resources for diagnosing needs, planning my learning, and learning; and to give help to them and receive help from them. | | | | |
| 4. The ability to diagnose my own learning needs realistically, with help from teachers and peers. | | | | |
| 5. The ability to translate learning needs into learning objectives in a form that makes it possible for their accomplishment to be assessed. | | | | |
| 6. The ability to relate to teachers as facilitators, helpers, or consultants, and to take the initiative in making use of their resources. | | | | |
| 7. The ability to identify human and material resources appropriate to different kinds of learning objectives. | | | | |
| 8. The ability to select effective strategies for making use of learning resources and to perform these strategies skillfully and with initiative. | | | | |
| 9. The ability to collect and validate evidence of the accomplishment of various kinds of learning objectives. | | | | |
| 10. | | | | |
| 11. | | | | |

**LEARNING RESOURCE C**

**LEARNING CONTRACT**

Name: John Doe

Learning Project: Self-Directed Learning

| 1 LEARNING OBJECTIVES | 2 LEARNING RESOURCES AND STRATEGIES | 3 EVIDENCE OF ACCOMPLISHMENT | 4 CRITERIA AND MEANS OF VALIDATING EVIDENCE |
|---|---|---|---|
| 1. To develop an understanding of the theory and practical implications of teacher-directed learning and self-directed learning. | Inquiry Projects 1, 2 & 3. Read Brown, Eble, Houle, and Tough. Learning Resource A. | A written or oral presentation of the definitions, rationales, assumptions, and required skills of each. | Make presentation to a high school student, college student, teacher, and adult friend and have them rate it on a 5-point scale as to: (1) clarity, (2) comprehensiveness, and usefulness to them. |
| 2. To enhance my self-concept as a self-directing person. | Learning Resource D. Inquiry Project 4. | Creating a satisfying learning contract. | Rating of the contract by two peers and a teacher as to degree of self-directedness it demonstrates. |
| 3. To gain skill in relating to peers collaboratively. | Learning Resource E. Learning Resource F. | Performance as a helper and helpee in a learning project with two or more peers. | Rating by the peers on my effectiveness as a helper and my openness to feedback as a helpee. |
| 4. To increase my skill in diagnosing my own learning needs. | Inquiry Projects 3 & 4. Learning Resource B. Learning Resource G. | Self-assessment as per Learning Resource G. | Rating by an expert on adequacy of model and accuracy of assessment. |
| 5. To increase my ability to translate learning needs into learning objectives. | Inquiry Projects 3 & 4. Learning Resource I. | Inquiry Project 4. | Rating by two peers and a teacher of objectives in contract as to measurability. |

| | | | |
|---|---|---|---|
| 6. To gain skill in making use of teachers as helpers and resources. | Inquiry Project 4. Learning Resource J. | Utilization of a teacher as a consultant and information source. | Rating by teacher used in Inquiry Project 4 of my skill in getting help and information. |
| 7. To increase my ability to identify human and material resources appropriate to different kinds of learning objectives. | Inquiry Project 4. | Resources identified in Inquiry Project 4. | Rating of resources by two peers and a teacher as to (1) variety, (2) appropriateness, (3) authoritativeness, and (4) feasibility. |
| 8. To increase my ability to select effective learning strategies. | Inquiry Project 4. Learning resource K. | Strategies identified in Inquiry Project 4. | Same as above. |
| 9. To increase my ability to collect and validate evidence of accomplishment of objectives. | Inquiry Project 4. Learning Resource N. Learning Resource O. | Identification of evidence and criteria and means of validation in Inquiry Project 4. | Rating of adequacy of evidence and criteria and means of validation by two peers and a teacher according to criteria of (1) appropriateness of objectives, (2) sufficiency, and (3) convincingness. |
| 10. | | | |
| 11. | | | |

# Learning Resource D

# The Self-Concept of a Self-Directing Person

It is suggested in Learning Resource B that one of the competencies possessed by self-directing learners is a concept of themselves as nondependent and self-directing persons. How does one develop such a self-concept? Certainly a starting point is having a clear picture of what it means—being able to visualize how you would feel, how you would think, what you would do if you were completely self-directing. Presented below are some descriptions of self-directed learners (or self-directed learning) that may help you construct a model for yourself and, by comparing where you are now in your thinking about yourself with that model, discover aspects of your self-concept that might need strengthening.

The adult able to break the habits of slovenly mentality and willing to devote himself seriously to study when study no longer holds forth the lure of pecuniary gain is, one must admit, a personality in whom many negative aims and desires have already been eliminated. Under examination, and viewed from the standpoint of adult education, such personalities seem to want among other things, intelligence, power, self-expression, freedom, creativity, appreciation, enjoyment, fellowship. Or, stated in terms of the Greek ideal, they are searchers after the good life. They want to count for something; they want their experiences to be vivid and meaningful; they want their talents to be utilized; they want to know beauty and joy; and they want all of these realizations of their total personalities to be shared in communities of fellowship. Briefly they want to improve themselves; this is their realistic and primary aim. But they want also to change the social order so that vital personalities will be creating a new environment in which their aspirations may be properly expressed.

—Eduard C. Lindeman, *The Meaning of Adult Education*
(New Republic, Inc., New York, 1926), pp. 13–14.

. . . if genuine dialogue is to arise, everyone who takes part in it must bring himself into it. And that also means that he must be willing on each occasion to say what is really in his mind about the subject of the conversation. And that means further that on each occasion he makes the contribution of his spirit without reduction and without shifting his ground. Even men of great integrity are under the illusion that they are not bound to say everything "they have to say." But in the great faithfulness which is the climate of genuine dialogue, what I have to say at any one time already has in me the character of something that wishes to be uttered, and I must not keep it back, keep it in myself.

—Martin Buber, "Elements of the Interhuman,"
translated by Ronald G. Smith, in *The Knowledge of Man*, edited by Maurice Friedman
(Harper and Row, Inc., New York, 1965.)

These populations [high learners] are marked by learning, by efforts to achieve their inherent potential, and by curiosity and joie de vivre. Yet, at the same time, these people like their present job, understand and accept their own characteristics, are not strongly dissatisfied with their present self. They have the confidence and courage to reveal their real self. They have clearly directed interests: they choose their own career and activities and are not pushed by external forces. They strive to achieve certain major goals, are spurred on rather than blocked by obstacles, and are productive and successful. Their relationship with at least a few people tends to be compassionate, loving, frank, and effective.

—Allen Tough, *The Adult's Learning Projects*
(Ontario Institute for Studies in
Education, Toronto, 1971), p. 28.

The school of the future must make the object of education the subject of his own education. The man submitting to education must become the man educating himself; education of others must become the education of oneself. This fundamental change in the individual's relationship to himself is the most difficult problem facing education for the future decades of scientific and technical revolution. (p. 161)

Learning to learn is not just another slogan. It denotes a specific pedagogic approach that teachers must themselves master if they want to be able to pass it on to others. It also involves the acquisition of work habits and the awakening of motivations which must be shaped in childhood and adolescence by the programmes and methods in schools and universities. Each individual's aspirations to self-learning must be realized by providing him—not only in school and university but elsewhere too, under conditions and circumstances of all kinds—with the means, tools, and incentives for making his personal studies a fruitful activity. (p. 209)

—Edgar Faure, and others, *Learning to Be*
(UNESCO, Paris, 1972).

The basic tenet of democracy has been stated in these terms: "When men are free, they can find their own best ways." But what is a free man? A man with a full belly? A man without problems? A man with no pressures? Free to do as he pleases? When such things are achieved, a man is still only part way there. People need more; they need the freedom to *become*. Scientists who have written about the nature of self-actualization are generally agreed that one characteristic of such fortunate persons is the possession of a high degree of self-esteem. They see themselves in essentially positive ways.

It would be hard, indeed, to overestimate the importance of a positive view of self for effective behavior. The self is the center of a person's existence, his frame of reference for dealing with life. Persons who approach their problems with an air of "can do" are already far ahead of those who begin with a "can't do" attitude, expecting defeat. With a positive view of self one can dare, be open to experience, and confront the world with open arms and quiet certainty.

> —Arthur W. Combs, Donald L. Avila, and
> William W. Purkey, *Helping Relationships:*
> *Basic Concepts for the Helping Professions*
> (Allyn and Bacon, Boston, 1971), p. 144.

A mature person is not one who has come to a certain level of achievement and stopped there. He is rather a *maturing* person—one whose *linkages with life* are constantly becoming stronger and richer because his attitudes are such as to encourage their growth rather than their stoppage. A mature person, for example, is not one who knows a large number of facts. Rather, he is one whose mental habits are such that he grows in knowledge and in the wise use of it. A mature person is not one who has built up a certain quota of human relationships—family, friends, acquaintances, fellow workers —and is ready to call a halt, dismissing the rest of the human race as unimportant. Rather, he is a person who has learned how to operate well in a human environment so that he continues both to add new people to those whom he cares about and to discover new bases of fellowship with those already familiar.

> —Harry A. Overstreet, *The Mature Mind*
> (W. W. Norton & Company, 1949), p. 43.

*(Cyril O. Houle, * in his pioneering study of continuing learners, found that they profited by seven key principles:)*

1. Act as though you are certain to learn. Nothing so disturbs the beginning adult student as the nagging fear that he will not be able to learn what he would like to learn. Nothing is more reassuring than the discovery through experience that he can succeed. . . . Adults can learn most things better than children, though it may take them longer to do so.

2. Set realistic goals—and measure their accomplishment. One frequent obstacle to adult learning is that men and women, realizing that they have the full power of their strength and vigor, think that they ought to be able to learn without any effort or strain whatever. . . . In any learning program, therefore, you must first of all be realistic about what you can achieve.

3. Remember the strength of your own point of view. Your learning is strongly influenced by the point of view you bring to it. . . . Most important of all, do not let your established values harden into such fixed beliefs that you cannot tolerate new ideas. When this happens, the process of education ceases.

4. Actively fit new ideas and new facts into context. Your greatest asset as an adult learner is the fact that your experience enables you to see relationships. When a new idea or fact is presented, you can understand it because you have background and perspective. And you can remember it because you can associate it with what you already know and therefore give it meaning.

5. Seek help and support when you need it. Sometimes an adult will choose to learn by himself, and sometimes he will choose to learn with others. A balanced learning program combines many elements, though not all at the same time. But while adults often teach themselves what they want to know, they may run into real dangers if they rely on this

* From *Continuing Your Education* by Cyril O. Houle. Copyright 1964 by McGraw-Hill Book Company. Used with permission of McGraw-Hill Book Company.

method too consistently. . . . One time when it is well to seek out a teacher is when you are beginning the study of a new subject. . . . A second time when you need help is when you bog down in your studies. . . . A third time when it is wise to seek help is when you feel the need of the social stimulation of a class or a group.

6. Learn beyond the point necessary for immediate recall. We all learn many things we do not really wish to remember—and which we promptly forget. . . . If you want to remember something permanently, however, you must do what the psychologist calls *over-learning*. Even after you can recall the fact or perform the skill perfectly, you should keep on reviewing it.

7. Use psychological as well as logical practices. You have already had an illustration of this rule. In Chapter 1 you were urged first to skim this book, then to read it, and then to examine it closely. Now it seems illogical to many people not to go through a book thoroughly, digesting a paragraph at a time. Yet research has shown that the way here recommended is better.

—Cyril O. Houle, *Continuing Your Education* (McGraw-Hill Book Company, New York, 1964), pp. 18–35.

Exploration of the full range of his own potentialities is not something that the self-renewing man leaves to the chances of life. It is something he pursues systematically, or at least avidly, to the end of his days. He looks forward to an endless and unpredictable dialogue between his potentialities and the claims of life—not only the claims he encounters but the claims he invents. And by potentialities I mean not just skills, but the full range of his capacities for sensing, wondering, learning, understanding, loving, and aspiring.

The ultimate goal of the educational system is to shift to the individual the burden of pursuing his own education. This will not be a widely shared pursuit until we get over our odd conviction that education is what goes on in school buildings and nowhere else. Not only does education continue when schooling ends, but it is not confined to what may be studied in adult education courses. The world is an incomparable classroom, and life is a memorable teacher for those who aren't afraid of her.

—John W. Gardner, *Self-Renewal*
(Harper & Row, New York, 1963), pp. 11–12.

It appears that the person who emerges from a theoretically optimal experience of personal growth, whether through client-centered therapy or some other experience of learning and development, is then a fully functioning person. He is able to live fully in and with each and all of his feelings and reactions. He is making use of all his organic equipment to sense, as accurately as possible, the existential situation within and without. He is using all of the data his nervous system can thus supply, using it in awareness, but recognizing that his total organism may be, and often is, wiser than his awareness. He is able to permit his total organism to function in all its complexity in selecting, from the multitude of possibilities, that behavior which in this moment of time will be most generally and genuinely satisfying. He is able to trust his organism in this functioning, not because it is infallible, but because he can be fully open to the consequences of each of his actions and correct them if they prove to be less than satisfying.

He is able to experience all of his feelings, and is afraid of none of his feelings; he is his own sifter of evidence, but is open to evidence from all sources; he is completely engaged in the process of being and becoming himself, and thus discovers that he is soundly and realistically social; he lives completely in this moment, but learns that this is the soundest living for all time. He is a fully functioning organism, and because of the awareness of himself which flows freely in and through his experiences, he is a fully functioning person.

—Carl R. Rogers, *Freedom to Learn*
(Charles E. Merrill Publishing Company,
Columbus, Ohio, 1969), p. 288.

# Learning Resource E
# Relationship-Building Exercises

*Rationale*

Students typically enter into any activity labeled "educational" with the notion that the appropriate relationship for them to establish with fellow students is that of competitor, and that they should relate to a teacher as an authority figure. This has been their conditioning, for the most part, through previous schooling. In Martin Buber's terms, they see one another as "its" rather than as "I's and thous," as objects rather than as fellow human beings. Furthermore, they tend to think of resources for learning as residing outside themselves—in teachers, experts, books, and the media. They usually don't even know what resources their fellow learners have to contribute, and wouldn't think of using these resources even if they knew what the resources were.

Self-directed learning can flourish only when learners and teachers see one another as mutually helpful human beings with resources to share.

*Objectives*

The objectives of these exercises are to help learners: (1) begin to experience other learners as collaborators rather than as competitors, as human beings rather than as

**71**

things; and (2) begin to identify the resources each learner needs from, and can provide to, other learners for their mutual learning. Which exercise you select will depend upon which one you feel most comfortable with and which you feel will fit best into the time limitations and the learners' moods.

### Exercise 1
(learner-initiated—30 minutes)

Identify one other learner you expect to relate to in a learning project and suggest that each of you take fifteen minutes to share (1) *what* you are—your work or student status, your background, what special resources you have that are relevant to this particular learning project; and (2) *who* you are—a few things that make you different from any other person, such as aspirations, feelings, needs, and values.

### Exercise 2
(teacher-initiated—45 minutes)

    a. Explain the rationale and objectives of this exercise.

    b. Ask the learners to form groups of five or six (in circles or around tables) and take five minutes each to share the following information: (1) *what* you are—your work or student status and what experiences, knowledge, or skills you have that are relevant to this particular learning situation; and (2) *who* you are—one thing about you that will help the others to see you as a unique human being.

    c. Before the groups start sharing, give the students the above information about yourself (and role model doing this within the five-minute time limit).

d. After the groups have completed their sharing, ask for a spontaneous reporting of the following information: (1) did anyone learn anything about someone else that was so unusual that others would be interested in knowing about it (be sure that permission is given by that person before it is reported), and (2) were any special resources uncovered that others would like to know about?

*Exercise 3*
(teacher-initiated—30 minutes)

a. Explain the rationale and objectives of this exercise.
b. Ask each student to take a sheet of 8½-by-11-inch paper, divide it into four equal boxes with pen or pencil lines, and write in a heading for each box as indicated below.

| I am ──<br><br>(1) What:<br><br><br>(2) Who: | I am feeling ── |
|---|---|
| I want help in ── | I can give help in ── |

    c. Ask each learner to take two minutes to write in each box the words or phrases that the heading of that box stimulates in his mind by free association. (Indicate when each two-minute period is up.)

    d. Ask the students to form groups of five or six (in circles or around tables) and take three minutes per box to share the words or phrases in each box. (Indicate when each three-minute period is up.)

    e. After the groups have completed their sharing, ask for spontaneous reporting of the following information: (1) what unusual information about the "what" and "who" of the members of the groups was surfaced; (2) what were the most frequent words in the "I am feeling" box; (3) what kinds of resources were identified as being needed; and (4) what kinds of help were identified as being available?

*Exercise 4*

(teacher-initiated—30 minutes)

    a. Explain the rationale and objectives of this exercise.

    b. Ask each student to take a large sheet of newsprint, masking tape, and felt pen, find a space on a wall to hang the sheet of paper, place his or her name at the top of the sheet, inscribe the form portrayed in Exercise 3, and write in the words or phrases he or she associates with each heading.

    c. As each student finishes, he or she walks around examining the sheets of other students and locates the students he or she identifies with or wants to know more about.

# Learning Resource F

# Consultation Skill-Practice Exercise

*Rationale*

One of the characteristics of self-directed learning is that learners give help to, and receive help from, one another. One kind of help that is exchanged is straight information giving and skill training, which is the kind of help we all have had most experience with.

Another kind of help is what has come to be called *"consultation."* Its purpose is to assist individuals to think through problems for themselves and to make their own decisions. It consists of guiding the *process* of problem-solving, and therefore is often called "process consultation." The ultimate outcome of a successful process consultation is not necessarily a better solution for the particular problem with which it is concerned, but rather greater confidence and more skill on the part of the individual who is being helped in solving his own problems. Thus, it is an educational activity more than a problem-solving activity, although the individual usually comes out with a better solution to the particular problem on which he is being consulted.

Most people have had less experience with this kind of helping role than with the information-giving kind of role, and therefore don't know how to do it as well.

*Objectives*

The objectives of this exercise are to provide the learner with: (1) some guidelines for performing the role of consultant; (2) some practice in performing this role, with feedback from an observer and a helpee; (3) some practice in making use of a consultant; and (4) some practice in performing the role of observer.

*Exercise*

    a. Explain the rationale and objectives of this exercise.

    b. Ask the participants to arrange themselves in triads quickly, picking people near them.

    c. Explain that you are going to assign a letter to each participant which he or she should remember, then go around the room pointing out an *A*, a *B*, and a *C* in each triad.

    d. Explain that in the next hour each person will have a brief experience performing the roles of helper, helpee, and observer, and that you are now going to make some suggestions about performing these roles.

    e. Pass out reproductions of the "Observer's Guide Sheet" portrayed at the end of this exercise and ask the learners to study it for a few moments.

    f. Point out that the behaviors listed on the left side of the sheet are those of the traditional "wise-uncle adviser," who sees his role as being to solve the problem *for* the helpee, whereas those on the right side are characteristic of the process consultant who sees his role as being to assist the helpee in solving his own problem. Invite any questions about the difference between the two kinds of behaviors, and clarify any confusions.

g. Suggest that when a participant is in the role of helper he or she try to exhibit the behaviors on the right side (and for reinforcement you may wish to review and perhaps illustrate the behaviors).

h. Suggest that when a participant is in the role of helpee he or she try to make use of the helper as a process consultant as skillfully as possible.

i. Suggest that when a participant is in the role of observer he or she jot down words or phrases in the appropriate box whenever he or she observes a behavior by the helper that seems to fit that box, so that the observer can recall that episode.

j. Explain that there will be three helper-helpee consultations of twelve minutes each, and that each one will be followed by an observer's report of four minutes.

k. Now ask each participant to take two or three minutes to think about a problem he or she would like help on (such as diagnosing his or her needs for learning in this course, stating objectives for a learning contract, dealing with an interpersonal conflict, and the like) and writing down on a slip of paper a one- or two-paragraph description of the problem.

l. Start Round 1 by asking the *A*'s in each triad

to take the role of helper, the *B*'s the role of helpee, and the *C*'s the role of observer.

m. At the end of twelve minutes call time and announce that the observer has four minutes to report his or her observations to the helper and helpee in his or her triad.

n. At the end of four minutes call time and start Round 2, in which *B* is the helper, *C* is the helpee, and *A* is the observer.

o. At the end of twelve minutes call time and ask the observers to give their feedback for four minutes.

p. At the end of four minutes call time and start Round 3, in which *C* is the helper, *A* is the helpee, and *B* is the observer.

q. At the end of twelve minutes call time and ask the observers to give their feedback for four minutes.

r. At the end of four minutes announce that the exercise is over, and that it is time to analyze the experience. Invite responses from the participants to such questions as:

(1) How did you feel playing the role of this kind of helper?

(2) At what points did you find it tempting to switch to the role of "wise-uncle advice-giver"? Why? What did you do about it?

(3) When you were a helpee, what kinds of things your helper did were especially helpful or hindering?

(4) When you were a helper, what kinds of things your helpee did were especially helpful or hindering?

(5) How useful was the feedback from the ob-

server? What kinds of observations were most (and least) helpful?

(6) How did you feel performing the role of observer? Now that you have had this experience, what would you do differently as an observer?

## RESOURCES FOR ADDITIONAL INQUIRY

Carkhuff, Robert R. *Helping and Human Relations*, Vol. II. New York: Holt, Rinehart and Winston, 1969, pp. 19–128.

Combs, Arthur W., Donald L. Avila, and William W. Purkey. *Helping Relationships*. Boston: Allyn and Bacon, 1971, pp. 210–231.

Rogers, Carl R. *On Becoming a Person*. Boston: Houghton Mifflin, 1961, pp. 31–58.

Schein, Edgar. *Process Consultation*. Reading, Mass.: Addison-Wesley, 1969, pp. 77–131.

## CONSULTATION EXERCISE

### Observer's Guide Sheet

Note instances in which the person you are observing in the "helping role":

*Versus*

| | |
|---|---|
| *Suggests* problems, facts, solutions, actions, etc. | *Asks* helpee for clarification of *his* perceptions, facts, solutions, etc. |
| *Interprets* helpee's feelings, motivations, inadequacies, etc. | *Seeks to understand* helpee's feelings, ideas, motivations, etc. |
| *Conveys doubts* about helpee's ability to cope with difficulty. | *Encourages and supports* helpee in using his abilities. |

# Learning Resource G

# Self-Assessment Exercise

## Rationale

Self-directed learning starts with learners becoming aware of some need for learning. This need may be to acquire some particular knowledge or skill in order to gain certain benefits, such as a better job or greater self-confidence, more self-esteem or greater competence in performing a role; or the need may be simply to enjoy the pleasure of learning or to satisfy a curiosity. In general, however, the clearer that learners are about their needs for learning in a particular situation the more efficiently can they plan their learning.

## Objectives

The objectives of this exercise are to help learners: (1) gain an understanding of the self-diagnostic process, and (2) have an exploratory experience in practicing this process.

### The Self-Diagnostic Process *

The diagnostic process involves three steps: (1) the development of a model of desired behaviors or required

* Adapted from Malcolm S. Knowles, *The Modern Practice of Adult Education: Andragogy versus Pedagogy* (New York: Association Press, 1970), pp. 273–284.

competencies; (2) the assessment of the present level of performance by the individual in each of these behaviors or competencies; and (3) the assessment of the gaps between the model and the present performance.

## I. DEVELOPING COMPETENCY MODELS

Models of desired behavior or required competence can be developed in several ways:

1. *Through research.*

   The Cooperative Extension Service, for example, has been able to develop rather specific models of the competencies required for successful farming by virtue of the research findings of state agricultural experiment stations regarding which practices produce the best crops. Many state extension services have conducted research on required competencies for many other roles as well, such as homemaker, youth leader, community-change agent, and farm business manager. Considerable research has been done by government agencies, industry, and the universities on competencies required for supervision and executive management—indeed, leadership in general. The competencies required by teachers, doctors, hospital administrators, nurses, social workers, and other professional roles have been subjects of a good deal of research But for most of the non-vocational roles that are central in the lives of human beings there is little research regarding required competencies.

2. *Through the judgments of experts.*

   The literature abounds with judgments of experts regarding the required competencies for performing a variety of roles, ranging from a wide range of occupations to leisure-time user. Many institutions make use of their own experts—their executives, personnel staff, supervisors, and field workers—to construct models of required competencies for roles unique to their particular institutions. For example, when the Girls Scouts of the U.S.A. decided to launch a new program of leadership training, they convened a conference of experts from various departments and levels of the organization who identified ten areas of required competencies for troop leaders. They then constructed "model statements" describing the general competencies required and listed specific behavior related to each competency.

3. *Through task analysis.*

   By means of more or less elaborate observations, time study, and record-keeping of several people actually performing a given role, it is possible to construct a model of the competencies possessed by the most effective performers. A good task analysis consists of a categorization of the situations encountered in a role and descriptions of the types of action and related competencies required to cope with these situations successfully. Such a task analysis can be made by people associated with a role, such as supervisors, colleagues, and subordinates, but its value is likely to be greater if made by more objective observers.

4. *Through group participation.*

   A fourth alternative is, of course, for a group to build its own model. And if time and circumstances permit, this is probably the alternative that will result in the greatest learning—for the process of building a model is itself a learning process, and the model that results, even though it will perhaps be cruder, is one to which the participants will have a deeper commitment. The sources of data available to a group in building its own model include (1) research findings and judgments of experts as reported in the literature, (2) observation by the participants of role models in the field, (3) presentations by experts in the classroom, (4) interviews by the participants of experts in the community, (5) the participants' own experiences and observations, and (6) the experience of the instructor and leaders of the sponsoring institution.

For the task of model-building to be manageable by a total group it is desirable that it be broken down into subtasks, with a separate team of participants for each subtask. For example, for a course on "Effective Human Relations," teams might be organized to develop lists of the required competencies of (a) knowledge, (b) insight, (c) attitude, (d) skill, (e) interest, and (f) value, for effective human-relations performance. The instructor would serve as a consultant and resource person to the teams in identifying sources of information about each type of required competence, and after a reasonable period of search the teams would pool their findings. For other subjects or roles a different set of subtasks may be desirable.

Any contemporary model developed early in an activity must, of course, be seen as being preliminary and tentative. As the participants learn more and more about their area of inquiry, their perception of required competencies will change. It is highly desirable, therefore, that the model be reviewed periodically during the activity.

It is important, too, if models are brought from the outside—from research, from task analysis, or from experts—that they be reviewed and tested by the participants so that they have the opportunity to modify or restate them and make them more their own.

## II. ASSESSING THE PRESENT LEVEL OF PERFORMANCE

Here we enter relatively new and unexplored territory in the technology of adult education. Because adult education was tied so closely to pedagogy for so long, little attention was given to developing procedures and tools for helping adults diagnose their own needs—after all, if the teachers already know what they need, why waste time getting the students into the act? So the reservoir of experience and materials for student self-diagnosis of present level of performance is extremely limited. Indeed, there is probably no aspect of the technology of adult education that is in greater need of creative contributions by innovative practitioners. But there has been enough experience by a few innovators in the last few years to give evidence of the fruitfulness of energy spent in this direction and to provide some helpful guidelines and procedures.

Because competition for grades is such a strong element in the tradition of education, most adults enter into a learning activity in a defensive frame of mind. One of their strongest impulses is to show how good they are. So the notion of engaging in a self-diagnostic process for the purpose of revealing one's weaknesses—one's need for additional learning—is both strange and threatening. It is crucial, therefore—particularly in the case of adults having their first andragogical experience—that ways be devised for helping participants get into a self-diagnostic frame of mind.

Certainly the establishment of a warm, supportive, non-threatening climate as described above is a prerequisite condition to beginning to work in this direction. I have found in my own experience that a brief presentation by the instructor of the rationale for self-diagnosis as an essential feature of self-directed learning helps to make the concept more intellectually acceptable—particularly if reinforced by the instructor's own example of seeking feedback regarding his own deficiencies.

Let us be clear about one thing before proceeding with this matter of assessing performance. We are not talking here about a highly precise mathematical process of quantitative measurement of the full range of behaviors required for performing any set of functions. Such an aspiration would be totally unrealistic given the present state of the human sciences—and perhaps, given the complexity of human nature, it always will be. Rather, we are talking about a process that is more sensitizing than measuring, more concerned with setting broad directions of growth rather than defining terminal behaviors. The purpose of the process we are concerned with here is to help an individual adult look objectively at his present level of performance of a relatively small sample of behaviors that are important to him at a given time in his development and to determine where he wants to invest energy in improving his performance in the light of his model of desired behaviors.

Different kinds of performance call for different kinds of assessment procedures. Performance assessment in the area of *knowledge* requires the participant to demonstrate in some way what he knows (or at least can recall). If the desired knowledge is in an established academic-subject field, or in any of several technical or vocational fields, one or more of the nationally standardized subject-knowledge tests may help a participant to assess his present level of performance. If a standardized test is not available, a teacher-made test could be used. But I have found student-made tests to be generally more acceptable and usually just as effective.

Performance assessment in the area of *understanding* and *insight* requires that a participant demonstrate his ability to size up situations, see patterns, develop categories, figure out cause-and-effect relationships, and in general to apply knowledge and thought processes to the analysis and solution of problems. Some standardized tests of critical-thinking ability are designed to give evidence regarding this type of performance, as are teacher-made essay tests. But adults are likely to find simulation exercises, in which they act out their understanding and insight in handling "live" problems, to be more realistic and relevant. For example, in a supervisory-training program groups of participants can take turns showing how they would handle various "critical incidents" supervisors typically face in dealing with subordinates, superiors, and colleagues; by comparing the various solutions tried and their effects, each trainee gets some insight into his understanding of these problems. Role playing and, on a more elaborate scale, business games are used for the same purpose.

Performance assessment in the area of *skills* requires that the participant do the action in question and have his proficiency rated in some way. A simple illustration of a skill-performance assessment procedure is provided by the device commonly used in public-speaking classes of having each participant make a short speech and having it rated by the other participants or a panel of speech experts on such scales as adequacy of vocabulary, clarity of expression, pacing, rhythm, gesturing, poise, conveying of sincerity, and other elements of the skill of speaking in public. The composite rating of the judges is then transposed onto a profile sheet, giving the participant a quick perspective on the areas of skill needing most improvement. Similar profiles can be drawn up from observer-ratings of performance in real or simulated situations for such other skills as machine operating, instruction giving, interviewing, discussion leading, delegating, conflict handling, decision-making, and any of the wide variety of skills involved in artistic and physical activities. For the assessment of certain basic skills, such as reading, computing, finger dexterity, etc., standardized tests are available.

Performance assessment in the areas of *attitudes, interests,* and *values* is much more difficult and even less precise than in the areas of knowledge, understanding, and skill. Some standardized tests exist that can be used to get verbalizations about self-perceived attitudes, interests, and values, but there is little assurance that these are the ones that will be acted on in a particular situation when the chips are down. Role playing, and especially reverse role playing (as when a white person takes the role of a black person and vice versa), has been used extensively in human-relations training to help individuals get insight into their attitudes as they are revealed in action. And decision-making exercises, in which the individual has to decide between two values (such as risky profit versus security), can help a person discover which values he chooses under pressure. But the technology has to advance much farther than it has before we can get very clear assessments in these areas.

## III. ASSESSMENT OF LEARNING NEEDS

The final step in the self-diagnostic process is for the individual to assess the gaps that exist between his model of desired behaviors and his present level of performance. In a few situations, where the competencies involved are fairly simple and mechanical, the profile of gaps (which, of course, represent needs for further learning) may be quite precise and complete. But in most situations this process of self-diagnosis is more artistic than scientific. It is, realistically, merely a way of helping an individual make more sensitive judgments about which of many possible directions he might take in his continuing self-development at a given time.

The fact is that the very idea of self-diagnosis by learners is so new that the tools and procedures for helping them do it are primitive and inadequate. Clearly, this will be an area of great technological ferment in the next few years and I urge my readers to put their creative energy to work on this great need and to share their innovations with me. For if one thing stands out about adult learning it is that a self-diagnosed need for learning produces much greater motivation to learn than does an externally diagnosed need.

*Exercise*

    a. Select some fairly simple competence you would like to improve your performance in, such as becoming a more polished public speaker (or swimmer, or golfer, or gardener, or dressmaker).

    b. Construct a model of the elements (knowledge, skills, attitudes) that constitute excellence in the performance of this competence. For example, in the case of public speaking, these elements might turn out to be as follows:

(1) A broad knowledge of the vocabulary used in a given subject-matter area.

(2) Skill in expressing one's ideas simply and clearly.

(3) Skill in pacing one's speech gracefully and with proper emphasis.

(4) The ability to project one's voice so that it can be heard distinctly by a large audience.

(5) The ability to organize one's presentation logically, with supportive facts, and with clarifying illustrations. And so on.

(6) It might be useful for you to check your list of elements with two or three experienced public speakers in order to get their ideas about the adequacy of your model.

c. Construct a rating scale, as illustrated below.

d. Make a speech and have it rated by the audience or by a panel of expert speakers.

e. Transpose the average of their ratings onto a rating scale sheet so that you end up with a profile showing your strengths and weaknesses in terms of your model, as follows:

# PROFILE OF RATINGS OF PUBLIC-SPEAKING COMPETENCIES

Performance Elements          Ratings

| Performance Elements | 1 | 2 | 3 | 4 | 5 | 6 | 7 | 8 | 9 | 10 |
|---|---|---|---|---|---|---|---|---|---|---|
| | Low | | | | | | | | | High |
| Vocabulary | | | | | | | | 8 | | |
| Clarity of expression | | | | | 5 | | | | | |
| Pacing, pausing, emphasis | | | 3 | | | | | | | |
| Voice projection | | | | 4 | | | | | | |
| Gesturing | | | | | | 6 | | | | |
| Logical development | | | | | | 6 | | | | |
| Adequacy of facts | | | | | | | 7 | | | |
| Adequacy of illustrations | | | | | | | | | | 10 |
| Appropriateness of humor | | | | | | 6 | | | | |
| Quality of opening | | | 3 | | | | | | | |
| Quality of closing | | | | 4 | | | | | | |
| Rapport with audience | | | 3 | | | | | | | |
| Conveying of sincerity | | | | | | | | 8 | | |
| Pronunciation | | | | 4 | | | | | | |
| Enunciation | | | | | 5 | | | | | |

# LEARNING RESOURCE H

## A CONTENT-COURSE SELF-ASSESSMENT INSTRUMENT

Course:  The Nature of Adult Education

Questions I Need to Inquire into Further

### Areas of Inquiry

The Role of Adult Education
in Society

1.  Its historical role

2.  Contemporary needs

3.  Aims of Adult Education
    as a movement

The Scope of Adult Education

1.  In terms of agencies

2.  In terms of content areas

3.  In terms of personnel

4.  In terms of program
    development

5.  In terms of methods

6.  In terms of materials

## Problems and Concerns in Adult Education

1. Coordination and role-clarification

2. Research and evaluation

3. Public understanding

4. Finance

5. Facilities

6. Philosophical issues

## Adult Education in Other Countries

## Trends and Strategies for the Future

# Learning Resources I

## Some Guidelines for Stating Objectives *

In actual educational practice, learning objectives are stated in many ways. All too often they are stated as things which the instructor or the activity is going to do, as, for example, "to give information about . . ." "to demonstrate . . ." "to broaden appreciation of . . ." or "to create an awareness of . . ." (These are, incidentally, direct quotes from activity announcements in my files.) These are not really statements of educational objectives, but rather of instructors' intentions. For education is not concerned with having the instructor perform certain activities; it is concerned with helping students achieve changes in behavior.

Objectives are sometimes stated in the form of lists of topics, concepts, or other content elements to be covered in an activity. Thus, a course in "Principles and Methods of Supervision" in a catalog in front of me at this moment

* Adapted from Malcolm S. Knowles, *The Modern Practice of Adult Education* (New York: Association Press, 1970), pp. 284–287.

states its objectives as being to cover "role and responsibility of supervisors; planning; defining tasks; establishing standards and controls; delegation of responsibility; communication; motivation and morale . . ." Objectives stated in the form of content elements may help students choose between activities, but they are not satisfactory learning objectives since they do not specify what the students are to do with the elements—memorize them, be able to apply them to life situations, feel differently about them, or what.

A third way in which objectives are often stated is in the form of generalized patterns of behavior without the content area to which the behavior applies being specified. For example, in front of me now is a brochure describing a library discussion program which states as its first objective "to develop critical thinking." But it doesn't say about what. Further down the list is "to develop broad interests" without any indication of the areas in which interests are to be aroused.

In my own practice I have found that it helps me to discipline myself to include both behavioral and content components if I use the phraseology "to develop . . . (in the sense of 'to help participants develop') in . . ." I have found it useful, also, to have a general typology of behavioral aspects of objectives as a frame of reference for organizing a set of objectives for an activity. Hilda Taba proposes the following typology:

> Knowledge: Facts, Ideas, Concepts
> Reflective Thinking
> —interpretation of data
> —application of facts and principles
> —logical reasoning
> Values and Attitudes

    Sensitivities and Feelings
    Skills *

A somewhat simpler typology is employed in the "Worksheet for Stating Learning Objectives" illustrated below, which I have used in some of my courses for developing specific statements of objectives collaboratively with my students. After the students have experienced some self-assessment such as that described in Learning Resource H, they are able to specify quite concretely the content areas in which they need behavioral changes of each of the five types. One of the advantages of organizing objectives according to a typology of this sort is that it provides direct guidance in the selection of techniques for each learning experience; for, as will be shown in Learning Resource K, certain techniques are more effective in helping students achieve certain objectives than are others.

The discussion of learning objectives up to this point has been in the broad humanistic sense of self-determined directions of self-development, with the instructor and the students participating mutually in the process of their formulation. But there is a rather substantial body of literature on objectives of a very different kind; and the discussion should not be ended without some acknowledgment of this other approach to the subject.

Programmed instruction is geared to a concept of "terminal behavior" objectives, with terminal behavior defined as "the behavior you would like your learner to be able to demonstrate at the time your influence over him ends." †
The specifications for this type of objective are summarized as follows:

* Hilda Taba, *Curriculum Development: Theory and Practice* (New York: Harcourt, Brace and World, 1962), pp. 211–28.
† Robert F. Mager, *Preparing Instructional Objectives* (Palo Alto, California: Fearon Publishers, 1962), p. 2.

1. A statement of instructional objectives is a collection of words or symbols describing one of your educational *intents*.

2. An objective will communicate your intent to the degree you have described what the learner will be DOING when demonstrating his achievement and how you will know when he is doing it.

3. To describe terminal behavior (what the learner will be DOING):

    a. Identify the name of the over-all behavior act.

    b. Define the important conditions under which the behavior is to occur (givens and/or restrictions and limitations).

    c. Define the criterion of acceptable performance.

4. Write a separate statement for each objective; the more statements you have, the better chance you have of making clear your intent.

5. If you give each learner a copy of your objectives, you may not have to do much else [*sic*].*

These statements are from a book entitled *Preparing Instructional Objectives*. But the educational philosophy expressed in the subtitle of the book—"A book for teachers and student teachers . . . for anyone interested in transmitting skills and knowledge to others"—explains why this approach to objectives is not given greater attention in this book about self-directed learning.

---

* *Ibid.*, p. 53. The *sic* means that this is precisely what the author says, but I doubt if he means what I suspect—that by this time the student, if he is an adult, will have disappeared.

```
                    WORKSHEET FOR STATING LEARNING OBJECTIVES

Behavioral Aspect                              Content Area
_____

                        1.
To develop knowledge    2.
  about:                3.
                        4.
                        5.
                        6.
                        7.
_____

                        1.
To develop under-       2.
  standing of:          3.
                        4.
                        5.
                        6.
                        7.
_____

                        1.
To develop skill        2.
  in:                   3.
                        4.
                        5.
                        6.
                        7.
_____

                        1.
To develop attitudes    2.
  toward:               3.
                        4.
                        5.
                        6.
                        7.
_____

                        1.
To develop values       2.
  of:                   3.
                        4.
                        5.
                        6.
                        7.
```

# Learning Resource J

# Questioning Strategies and Techniques

Self-directed learning means learners engaging in inquiry. Inquiry means getting answers to questions through the collection and analysis of data. The prerequisite skill of inquiry, therefore, is the ability to formulate questions that can be answered by data.

Unfortunately, this is a skill that few of us have learned through our schooling. Rather, we have been taught to ask questions that can be answered by authority (a teacher, a textbook) or by faith. For example, "What grade will the teacher give me?" is a question that can be answered only by authority; "Will the teacher grade fairly?" is a question that usually can be answered only by faith; "What will be the effect on my grade of two different ways of studying," however, is a question that can be answered through inquiry (using an experimental design).

## DESIGNING A PLAN OF INQUIRY

A plan of inquiry involves asking six specific process questions and testing their adequacy against certain criteria, as follows:

1. What is the question you want to get an answer to? With the criteria of adequacy being:
   a. Is it a question worth asking?
   b. Is it a question you really care about?
   c. Is it a question that is answerable by data?
   d. Is the question clear and understandable to others?

2. What data are required to answer this question? With the criteria of adequacy being:
   a. Have subquestions requiring different kinds of data been identified?
   b. Are you clear about the data required to answer this particular question and no other?
   c. Are these data available to you within your limitations of time, money, etc.?

3. What are the sources of the required data? With the criteria of adequacy being:
   a. Are the sources feasible for you, *i.e.*, within your reach and competence?
   b. Are the sources reliable and authentic repositories of the particular data you require?
   c. Are the requirements for data from primary versus secondary sources clearly delineated?

4. What means will be used to collect the data? With the criteria of adequacy being:
   a. Are these the most efficient and effective means for collecting these particular data from these sources?
   b. Are the means within your competence to use, or do you need further training for them?
   c. Will these means produce reliable and valid data?
   d. Will they produce data that will answer the question you are asking?

5. How will the data be analyzed so as to answer the question you are asking?
   With the criteria of adequacy being:
   a. Are the methods of analysis within your competence to use, or do you require further training for them?
   b. Will these methods of analysis produce a clear and significant answer to the specific question raised?
   c. Are these the most efficient and relevant methods of analysis for the data provided and the question posed?
6. How will the answer to the question be presented?
   a. Will the answer be clearly supported by the data?
   b. Is this form of presentation the most efficient and understandable possible?

## SOME SKILL PRACTICE IN QUESTIONING TECHNIQUES *

Students can learn a great deal about questions and their effective use from just being allowed opportunities to formulate some and carry out investigations of them. However, informal learning about questions should not exclude formal instruction. Students can have periods of time designated for focusing on their process of inquiry or problem-solving. Such focus would naturally deal with questions. Here students can analyze the types of questions they have been asking. Are they satisfied with their questions? Have they considered their questions produc-

* Reprinted, with permission, from Francis P. Hunkins, *Questioning Strategies and Techniques* (Boston: Allyn and Bacon, 1972). pp. 73–75.

tive in directing them to designated goals? What is the type of question they most commonly formulate?

Students who are presented opportunities to inquire within the discovery curriculum will most likely develop felt needs for formal discussion of questions. Students who are active in learning need to have time scheduled for analyzing just how they proceed. We can discuss with students the several types of questions according to some guide such as Bloom.* We should be sure that it is a guided discussion rather than just an exposition. We can present for discussion the idea that various types of questions will provide certain types of data. We might direct consideration as to what students do in questioning when they wish to formulate a generalization.

Before commencing formal discussion of questions, the teacher assigns students the task of listing some of the major questions they used in dealing with particular research topics. This list can then be considered in class group discussion. Students can analyze and criticize the different questions listed. Just what are the characteristics of the many questions asked? Why do you suppose this question was asked? If a student wished to develop a generalization, should he have asked primarily comprehension questions?

Such focus on questions also can lead to a consideration of the numerous questioning strategies the students used. Students engaged in oral investigation with a team partner might record their questions as they consider data. The tapes could then be studied to check if certain types of questions were used at the beginning of the inquiry and other types at the end. Where did the student put his most

* The reference is to Benjamin S. Bloom, ed. *Taxonomy of Educational Objectives, Handbook I: The Cognitive Domain* (New York: McKay, 1956).

significant questions in relation to his search? Did he comprise a list of significant questions to search for, or did he just react to specific types of data and then draw questions from this experience?

. . . . . . . . . . . . . . . . . . . . .

Students also should have time for practicing at writing various types of questions and for judging the questions of others. Students can be grouped in teams of two and use each other as sounding boards regarding their questions. Perhaps the class can develop certain guides in formulating the several types of questions. The development of criteria for effective questions can be a class task. Here students could do some reading of the question and its importance. Students could read about inquiry in articles published in school magazines.

Related to writing diverse questions is being able to identify questions in written materials. Students, perhaps in teams, can analyze questions in textbooks and various supplementary books. Such analysis could focus on the intent of the questions. Also, if students wished to gain information other than that asked for in the material, what types of questions would they have to state?

# LEARNING RESOURCE K

## RELATING METHODS TO OBJECTIVES*

| Type of Objectives | Most Appropriate Methods |
|---|---|
| KNOWLEDGE<br><br>(Generalizations about experience; internalization of information). | Lecture, television, debate, dialogue, interview, symposium, panel, group interview, colloquy, motion picture, slide film, recording, book-based discussion, reading, programmed instruction. |
| UNDERSTANDING<br><br>(Application of information and generalizations). | Audience participation, demonstration, dramatization, Socratic discussion, problem-solving project, case method, critical incident process, simulation games. |
| SKILLS<br><br>(Incorporating new ways of performing through practice). | Skill practice exercises, role-playing, in-basket exercises, participative cases, simulation games, human relations training groups, nonverbal exercises, drill, coaching. |
| ATTITUDES<br><br>(Adoption of new feelings through experiencing greater success with them than with old feelings). | Experience-sharing discussion, sensitivity training, role-playing, critical incident process, case method, simulation games, participative cases, group therapy, counseling. |
| VALUES<br><br>(The adoption and priority arrangement of beliefs). | Value-clarification exercises, biographical reading, lecture, debate, symposium, colloquy, dramatization, role-playing, critical incident process, simulation games, sensitivity training. |

*Adapted from Malcolm S. Knowles, *The Modern Practice of Adult Education* (New York: Association Press, 1970), p.294.

# Learning Resource L

# Exercise in Reading a Book Proactively

*Rationale*
Self-directed learning implies that learners take the initiative in making use of resources, rather than simply react to transmissions from the resources. They know what they want to get from a resource, and they probe the resource until they get what they want. They are proactive rather than reactive learners.

But most of us have developed the habit of using resources—especially books—reactively. We start reading a book on page one and read it through to the end, letting the author tell us the answers to the questions he or she thinks we *ought* to be asking. Of course, some books have to be read this way. Most works of fiction, creative essays, and philosophical essays develop plots or themes with sequential elements. But most books that we turn to for information, such as textbooks, reference books, manuals, and anthologies, are organized according to content categories. Readers who know the questions to which they want answers can turn to the content category containing the answers to *their* questions. The book then takes on a different character; rather than being a one-way transmission of information, it is a resource for self-directed inquiry.

*Objectives*

The objectives of this exercise are to help the learner
(1) gain an understanding of the concept of proactive use
of resources, and (2) have an initial experience in practicing the skills of reading a book proactively.

*Exercise*

   a. In the advance announcement of the meeting
      at which this exercise is to be conducted, ask
      the participants to bring with them an informa-
      tional book that has a dust jacket, table of con-
      tents, and index. (It is wise for the teacher to
      bring a small supply of books for those partici-
      pants who neglect to bring a book.)
   b. In opening the session, explain the rationale
      and objectives of the exercise.
   c. It adds zest to the exercise if you suggest that
      each participant exchange his or her book with
      another participant, so that each is working
      with an unfamiliar book.
   d. Ask the participants to take the following steps:
      (1) Turn to the front of the dust jacket and
          read what the publisher has to say about
          the purpose of the book.
      (2) Turn to the rear of the dust jacket and
          read what the publisher has to say about
          the author and his or her qualifications to
          write such a book.
      (3) Turn to the front matter (introduction,
          foreword, preface) and read the author's
          or editor's orientation to the book.
      (4) Turn to the table of contents and see how
          the author has organized the information

into chapters, subsections, or other content categories.

(5) Put the book down, get out a sheet of paper, and write down three questions about things you have become curious about as a result of this preliminary examination of the book.

(6) Now that you have thought of three questions, review the first question and find in it a key word or phrase that you think might be in the book's index.

(7) Turn to the index and look up that key word or phrase. If the word or phrase is not there, think of a synonym and see if the synonym is there. If it isn't, then see if the table of contents can lead you to the page of the book where the question can be answered.

(8) Now turn to that part of the book that deals with your question and get the answer. If the author refers to material in other parts of the book, follow his leads until you have all the information relevant to your question.

(9) If time allows, follow the same procedure with the second and third questions.

e. Now engage the participants in an analysis of their experience. Such questions as the following usually produce deepened insights:

(1) How differently did you feel about using a book as a resource from the way you usually feel about reading a book?

(2) Is there any difference in the quality of the information you have gained?

# Learning Resource M

# Exercise in Using Human Resources Proactively

*Rationale*
The rationale for this exercise is the same as for Learning Resource L.

*Objectives*
The objectives of this exercise are to help the learner (1) gain an understanding of the concept of proactive use of human resources, and (2) have an initial experience in practicing the skills of using a human resource proactively.

*Exercise*
    a. If this exercise is not being conducted in conjunction with Learning Resource L, explain the rationale, given in Learning Resource L, and the above objectives.
    b. Ask each participant to pair off with one of the other participants he or she knows least about.
    c. Ask the participants in each pair to take fifteen minutes each describing to the other what he or

she perceives to be the principal resources he or she possesses (as a result of experiences, previous training, reading, etc.) that might be useful to others.

d. Ask each participant to take five minutes to formulate three questions he or she would like to get answers to from his or her partner.

e. Give each participant fifteen minutes to get the answers to his or her questions from the partner.

f. Engage the participants in an analysis of the experience by asking questions similar to those in Learning Resource L.

# Learning Resource N
# Types of Evidence
# for Different Objectives

Different types of evidence are required for assessing the accomplishment of different objectives. The examples below may provide guidance in thinking of ways you might go about getting evidence that is appropriate for your objectives.

| Objective | Types of Evidence |
|---|---|
| KNOWLEDGE | Reports of knowledge acquired, as in essays, examinations, oral presentations, audiovisual presentations. |
| UNDERSTANDING | Examples of utilization of knowledge in solving problems, as in critical incident cases, simulation games, proposals of action projects, research projects with conclusions and recommendations. |
| SKILLS | Performance exercises, with ratings by observers. |

| | |
|---|---|
| **ATTITUDES** | Attitudinal rating scales; performance in role playing, critical incident cases, simulation games, sensitivity groups, etc., with feedback from observers. |
| **VALUES** | Value rating scales; performance in value clarification groups, critical incident cases, simulation games, etc., with feedback from observers. |

# Learning Resource O

# Some Examples of Rating Scales

The instruments reproduced on the next few pages are examples of rating scales that were constructed by students in one of my courses (ED 559E: Adult Learning) to collect or validate evidence of accomplishment of various objectives.

They are presented here in the hope that they may stimulate ideas for constructing your own instruments.

```
                    EVALUATION

COURSE:_____

LEARNER:_____

EVALUATOR:  Inquiry Group

OBJECTIVE 1: To develop a better understanding of cur-
             rent learning concepts and theories.

LEARNING STRATEGY: To attend class regularly and to
                   participate in class activities and
                   discussions.

                                        Low        High

1. Was my participation adequate?       1  2  3  4  5

2. Were my questions relevant to
   the discussion?                      1  2  3  4  5

3. Did I take up too much class time
   for my own observations and remarks? 1  2  3  4  5

4. Did I help other class members by
   evaluating them when asked to do so? 1  2  3  4  5

5. Was my attendance at class meetings
   regular?                             1  2  3  4  5
```

EVALUATION

COURSE: _____

LEARNER: _____

EVALUATOR:  Inquiry Group

OBJECTIVE 2: To develop knowledge of the changes adults, particularly those over 60 years of age, experience as they develop.

LEARNING STRATEGY: To read in various sources about people over sixty; to conduct and tape interviews with three people in this age group and with the director of a program of volunteer community service for retired senior citizens.

|  | Low |  |  | High |  |
|---|---|---|---|---|---|
| 1. Is my reading list appropriate for a study of people over sixty? | 1 | 2 | 3 | 4 | 5 |
| 2. Was the reading material useful in the preparation of the group presentation? | 1 | 2 | 3 | 4 | 5 |
| 3. Was my participation in the preparation of the interviewer's guide helpful to the group? | 1 | 2 | 3 | 4 | 5 |
| 4. Were the interviews appropriate methods of study for learning about people over sixty? | 1 | 2 | 3 | 4 | 5 |
| 5. Were the interviews useful in the preparation of the class presentation? | 1 | 2 | 3 | 4 | 5 |

EVALUATION

COURSE: _____

LEARNER: _____

EVALUATOR: Consultation Group

OBJECTIVE 3: To develop technical skill in using new methods and techniques for the class presentation.

LEARNING STRATEGY: To take photographs of people interviewed; to help select other visual material for slides; to help prepare the tape for the narrator; to help coordinate the slides and sound.

|  | Low | | | High | |
|---|---|---|---|---|---|
| 1. Were the photographs appropriate for the program? | 1 | 2 | 3 | 4 | 5 |
| 2. Were the photographs useful to the program? | 1 | 2 | 3 | 4 | 5 |
| 3. Was the recording of the "rough" tape for the narrator a contribution to the group project? | 1 | 2 | 3 | 4 | 5 |
| 4. Was the help I gave in coordinating the sound and visuals valuable to the group? | 1 | 2 | 3 | 4 | 5 |
| 5. Do you think I developed new skills in this learning experience? | 1 | 2 | 3 | 4 | 5 |

### EVALUATION

COURSE:_____

LEARNER:_____

EVALUATOR:  Consultation Group

OBJECTIVE 5:   To develop knowledge of various theories
of learning in attempting to construct a
personal theory of learning.

LEARNING STRATEGY:  To read B. F. Skinner's *Beyond
Freedom and Dignity*; to review a video
tape of Arthur Combs presenting *The
Humanistic Approach*; to read Coolie
Verner and Catherine Davison's *Physio-
logical Factors in Adult Learning and
Instruction*; to read Verner and Davi-
son's *Psychological Factors in Adult
Learning and Education*.

|  | Low |  |  |  | High |
|---|---|---|---|---|---|
| 1. Do you think that as a novice in the field of learning theory that I selected an appropriate range of materials to review? | 1 | 2 | 3 | 4 | 5 |
| 2. Do my notes indicate diligent perusal of the materials? | 1 | 2 | 3 | 4 | 5 |
| 3. Are the notes in readable form? | 1 | 2 | 3 | 4 | 5 |
| 4. Do the notes appear to be useful for future reference and review? | 1 | 2 | 3 | 4 | 5 |

### SCALE USED FOR CLASS EVALUATION BY INQUIRY GROUP

What changes do adults experience as they develop, and how does this affect adult learning?

Instructions: For items A(1-4) and B, place an X at the point you feel you currently are. *Do not make any other marks until you are given further instructions.*

#### I. CONTENT

A. To what extent do you understand the effect of aging on the following:

   **1. PHYSICAL CAPACITIES**

| | | | | | | |
|---|---|---|---|---|---|---|

   Little                                  **Great**
   Understanding                         **Understanding**

   **2. MENTAL ABILITIES**

| | | | | | | |
|---|---|---|---|---|---|---|

   Little                                  **Great**
   Understanding                         **Understanding**

   **3. ATTITUDES AND VALUES**

| | | | | | | |
|---|---|---|---|---|---|---|

   Little                                  **Great**
   Understanding                         **Understanding**

   **4. INTERESTS**

| | | | | | | |
|---|---|---|---|---|---|---|

   Little                                  **Great**
   Understanding                         **Understanding**

B. To what extent do you feel a need to consider the above referenced items in planning for adult learning?

| | | | | | | |
|---|---|---|---|---|---|---|

   None                                   **Very Much**

**C.** The content of the presentation by the Inquiry Group

|  | Yes | To Some Extent | No |
|---|---|---|---|
| - presented new material, | ____ | ____ | ____ |
| - was too general for me, | ____ | ____ | ____ |
| - was too valuable for practical application, | ____ | ____ | ____ |
| - was too theoretical, | ____ | ____ | ____ |
| - gave me some new ideas or insight which will help, | ____ | ____ | ____ |
| - was too elementary, | ____ | ____ | ____ |
| - opened some new areas of inquiry which I might like to pursue. | ____ | ____ | ____ |

## II. METHOD OF PRESENTATION

**A.** On the scale below, rate the method of presentation for its originality and creativity, i.e., the degree to which it was fresh, new and/or novel.

Low                                                                High

**B.** The organization of the materials in this presentation was

(check one)

____ weak and needs improvement

____ average

____ above average but room for improvement

____ excellent with little room for improvement

EVALUATION

Evaluation of _____

Name _____

Date of Evaluation _____

Evaluated by _____

Objective: To develop a greater comprehension of the effects of aging in respect to learning that middle adults experience.

For each of the items listed below, indicate on the scale where you feel the person being rated falls.

1. How appropriate were materials read to the group activity?

Low | | | | | | High
     1   2   3   4   5

2. How useful were materials gathered to the group activity?

Low | | | | | | High
     1   2   3   4   5

3. How creatively were materials used in presentation?

Low | | | | | | High
     1   2   3   4   5

4. How useful were taped interviews of middle adults?

Low | | | | | | High
     1   2   3   4   5

5. How well do you think this group member understands the effects of aging on physical capacity, mental capacity, interests, attitudes of adults?

Low | | | | | | High
     1   2   3   4   5

6. How helpful do you think this group member was to the over-all presentation?

Low | | | | | | High
     1   2   3   4   5

EVALUATION OF PROCESS DESIGN

Evaluation of _____

Name _____

Date of Evaluation _____

Evaluated by _____

Objective: To develop skill in constructing a process design.

For each of the items listed below, indicate on the scale where you feel the person being rated falls.

1. How relevant are inquiry units?

   Low |___|___|___|___|___| High
        1   2   3   4   5

2. How clearly are problems stated?

   Low |___|___|___|___|___| High
        1   2   3   4   5

3. How appropriate are the resources listed?

   Low |___|___|___|___|___| High
        1   2   3   4   5

4. How useful is design as a tool for developing more self-directed learners?

   Low |___|___|___|___|___| High
        1   2   3   4   5

## PRESENTATION OF HUMANISTIC THINKING: EVALUATION

Evaluation of _____

Name _____

Date of Evaluation _____

Evaluated by _____

Objective: To develop knowledge of humanistic thinking and to integrate insights gained into a personal theory of learning.

For each of the items listed below, indicate on the scale where you feel the person being rated falls.

1. How clearly were the ideas presented?

   Low |___|___|___|___|___| High
        1   2   3   4   5

2. How relevant are ideas presented to the teaching-learning process?

   Low |___|___|___|___|___| High
        1   2   3   4   5

3. How well did presenter analyze differences between behaviorist and humanistic thinking?

   Low |___|___|___|___|___| High
        1   2   3   4   5

4. How useful are ideas presented to the development of a personal learning theory?

   Low |___|___|___|___|___| High
        1   2   3   4   5

EVALUATION OF THE ADULT'S LEARNING PROJECT

Student: _____

Course: _____

Objective: To better understand the implications and applica-
tions of humanism in education.

Learning Strategy: Completion of Allen Tough's *The Adult's
Learning Projects*

Evaluation: After looking over the notes and reading the paper
on Tough's book:

**1.** Do you feel that this was an appropriate task to meet
the objective?

|  |  |  |
|---|---|---|
| ☐ | ☐ | ☐ |
| No | Somewhat | Yes |

**2.** Were the notes readable, stressing the author's main
and important points?

|  |  |  |
|---|---|---|
| ☐ | ☐ | ☐ |
| No | Somewhat | Yes |

**3.** Was the written work comprehensive and clear in establishing the personal feelings of the student as
related to the book?

|  |  |  |
|---|---|---|
| ☐ | ☐ | ☐ |
| No | Somewhat | Yes |

**4.** Did the notes and paper show an understanding of the
concepts the book deals with?

|  |  |  |
|---|---|---|
| ☐ | ☐ | ☐ |
| No | Somewhat | Yes |

**5.** Do you feel that the written work will serve as a
useful future resource to the student?

|  |  |  |
|---|---|---|
| ☐ | ☐ | ☐ |
| No | Somewhat | Yes |

Signature:_____

## LEARNING EXPERIENCE EVALUATION

I would like to ask you to take a few minutes to respond to the following statements in order to help me evaluate the learning experience we have just been involved in together. I will use the responses I receive from you as one source of information to improve my own abilities in planning future learning experiences.

Circle the letter before the phrase which best expresses your thoughts about this learning experience. Please answer *all* questions.

1. During the experience I felt

    a. dependent upon the leader for planning the activity

    b. responsible for directing some of the activity

2. I thought the leader

    a. had an authoritarian attitude toward me

    b. respected me as an equal

3. The atmosphere was

    a. formal

    b. informal

4. I felt the material was planned to cover

    a. certain specified topics

    b. problem areas I needed to deal with

5. During the experience, I felt I was treated as

    a. a child

    b. an adult

## MOTIVATION AND LEARNING EVALUATION

Evaluation of paper submitted by _____
on the subject of "Motivation and Learning."

|                                                              | Low |   |   | High |   |
|--------------------------------------------------------------|-----|---|---|------|---|
| Adequacy of sources.                                         | 1   | 2 | 3 | 4    | 5 |
| Comprehensiveness.                                           | 1   | 2 | 3 | 4    | 5 |
| Clarity of ideas and expression.                             | 1   | 2 | 3 | 4    | 5 |
| Organization and logical development of material.            | 1   | 2 | 3 | 4    | 5 |
| Ability to *orally* apply schematic concept to a learning situation. | 1   | 2 | 3 | 4    | 5 |

Comments: _____

_____

_____

_____

                                        _____
                                           Evaluator

## EVALUATION OF PRESENTATION

Evaluation of summaries regarding factors which inhibit participation of adults in learning situations and recommended methods and techniques which are likely to assist in overcoming them.

|                                                                                              | Low |   |   | High |   |
|----------------------------------------------------------------------------------------------|-----|---|---|------|---|
| Usefulness of information.                                                                    | 1   | 2 | 3 | 4    | 5 |
| Ability to summarize findings.                                                               | 1   | 2 | 3 | 4    | 5 |
| Ability to orally present findings.                                                          | 1   | 2 | 3 | 4    | 5 |
| Understanding of underlying causes.                                                          | 1   | 2 | 3 | 4    | 5 |
| Understanding of the reasons for using recommended techniques – or rationale for not using those recommended. | 1   | 2 | 3 | 4    | 5 |

Comments: _____

_____

_____

_____

Evaluator

### EVALUATION OF PRESENTATION

TOPIC: The Role of the Teacher                    Date: _____

Please read the following statements and in each one circle the
phrase that best describes your reaction to tonight's presentation:

1. During this presentation I learned:

   *nothing new    a little    some    quite a lot    a great deal*

2. The effectiveness of presenting material through a panel com-
   posed of human resources was:

   *not good    poor    average    very good    excellent*

3. Opportunity for class participation was:

   *not at all    a little    somewhat    quite a bit    completely open*

4. My interest in the subject matter has been increased:

   *not at all    a little    somewhat    quite a bit    extremely*

Comments: _____

_____

_____

_____

_____

_____

_____

_____

_____

*NOTE:* Descriptors rated using
following criterion:

                Rating (5=High)
                1    2    3    4    5

EVALUATION OF A TEACHER

A thoughtful student reaction can help improve teaching effectiveness. Your careful answers to these questions will be greatly appreciated. Please check the rating you think applies to the teacher, the content, and your participation in this course.

|  | Not at All | Some-what | Average | A Great Deal |
|---|---|---|---|---|
| 1. To what extent were you familiar with the content of this course before the beginning of the quarter? | ___ | ___ | ___ | ___ |
| 2. To what extent do you see this course as being necessary to your major area of study? | ___ | ___ | ___ | ___ |
| 3. Which term best describes the degree of your knowledge of the subject matter gained so far in this course? | ___ | ___ | ___ | ___ |
| 4. To what degree has participation in this course increased your desire to learn more about the subject? | ___ | ___ | ___ | ___ |

If you desire, explain or comment on your replies to Numbers 1, 2, 3, 4.

_____

_____

5. To what extent does this instructor:

| | | | | |
|---|---|---|---|---|
| a. Encourage and respect students rights to express opinions different from his/her own? | ___ | ___ | ___ | ___ |
| b. Appear to understand students' feelings and problems? | ___ | ___ | ___ | ___ |
| c. Tell or show students they have done particularly well? | ___ | ___ | ___ | ___ |
| d. Show interest in and/or enthusiasm for this subject? | ___ | ___ | ___ | ___ |
| e. Use examples or illustrations to clarify the material covered in the text or lectures? | ___ | ___ | ___ | ___ |
| f. Plan with the students for an effective learning experience during this course? | ___ | ___ | ___ | ___ |
| g. Try to find the best ways to help each individual student learn? | ___ | ___ | ___ | ___ |

**h.** Make clear and follow through on the objectives for this course? _____ _____ _____ _____

**i.** Make clear the method of evaluating students' work? _____ _____ _____ _____

If you desire, please explain or comment on your replies to Number 5.

_____

_____

6. To what degree have you as a student in this course taken responsibility for the following:

**a.** Willingness to be a self-motivated learner? (For example: doing more than just work assigned by instructor, learning to work with less supervision, selecting own projects when possible.) _____ _____ _____ _____

**b.** Giving enough time to the course in reading, individual and class projects, etc.? _____ _____ _____ _____

**c.** Trying to develop a positive attitude toward this course? _____ _____ _____ _____

**d.** Trying to develop a positive attitude toward this instructor? _____ _____ _____ _____

**e.** Being actively involved in participation in

(1) helping to plan the course activities? _____ _____ _____ _____

(2) helping to evaluate your own work in the course? _____ _____ _____ _____

If you desire, please explain or comment on your replies to Number 6.

_____

_____

7. If you were able to change this course in any way, what constructive suggestions do you have for making the learning experience more meaningful and beneficial for you and other students? Please be as specific as possible in your recommendations.

Comments: _____

_____

_____

# Appendix

# Guidelines for Contract Learning

Many students find that the idea of constructing learning contracts for the first time is so strange that they become over-anxious. They have been so conditioned to having teachers tell them what they are to learn and how they are to learn it that they become confused and worried when confronted with the responsibility of thinking through what they want to learn and how they will go about learning it. These guidelines have been developed in the hope that they will facilitate your entering into this process with more security and greater ease.

## Why Contract Learning?

One of the most significant findings from research about adult learning (see, for example, Allen Tough's *The Adult's Learning Projects*) is that when adults go about learning something naturally (as contrasted with being taught), they are highly self-directing. Evidence is accumulating that what adults learn on their own initiative they learn more deeply a
nently than what they learn by being taught. In fa
strong evidence from both psychotherapeutical and

mental psychological research that a prime characteristic of adultness is the need and capacity to be self-directing.

But it is a fact of life that when an individual enters into certain educational situations, such as professional preparation, given requirements are imposed on him. The profession itself—as represented by licensing boards, certification standards, and acceptance by peers—specifies that certain knowledges, skills, attitudes, and values must have been acquired as a condition for admission to the profession. Colleges and universities spell out minimum standards of achievement as conditions for awarding their degrees.

The learning contract is a means of reconciling these "imposed" requirements from institutions and society with the learners' need to be self-directing. It enables them to blend these requirements in with their own personal goals and objectives, to choose their own ways of achieving them, and to measure their own progress toward achieving them. The learning contract thus makes visible the mutual responsibilities of the learner, the teacher, and the institution.

### How do you develop a learning contract?

*Step 1.* In the opening session of the course you will be given a syllabus which contains *a)* a list of the "given" objectives of the course, *b)* a list of references containing information relevant to these objectives, and *c)* a list of "inquiry units" specifying the kinds of questions with which the course deals. The course instructor will review these elements and dialogue with you for clarification and understanding. You have the responsibility to take the initiative in probing to eliminate any confusion at this point.

Between the first and the second sessions you will have the responsibility of familiarizing yourself with the territory the course is designed to explore—scan the literature, talk with people who are experienced in the field of study, and reflect on your own model of excellence for yourself. In this step you are developing *your* model of competencies (knowledges, skills, attitudes, and values) regarding the content of the course—a model which includes the objectives given in the syllabus that are relevant to you plus your own personal objectives that go beyond those given in the syllabus.

*Step 2.* In the second session you will be given a set of blank contract forms along with some examples of contracts from previous courses. Notice that the contract forms include one form for a *B*-level contract and one form for an *A*-level contract. You may contract for a *B* only, if you wish. But if you wish to contract for an *A*, both the *B*-level and the *A*-level forms are to be filled out.

What is the difference between a *B*-level and an *A*-level contract? A *B*-level contract is based on the accomplishment of the "given" objectives contained in the syllabus, on the assumption that these describe the core content of the course that *all* students should acquire in order to be able to perform adequately in this aspect of the field. An *A*-level contract, however, should specify objectives over and above these "generalist" objectives; it should describe learnings that would enable you to perform with *distinction* in one or more aspects of the. content. The difference, in short, is between "adequate" accomplishment and "distinguished" accomplishment. Whether or not your contract achieves this difference acceptably is a matter for negotiation between you and the instructor—with consultation from your peers.

Now you are ready to start filling out the first column of the contract form—"Learning Objectives." Start with the *B*-level contract. First, review the objectives in the syllabus. You may already have accomplished one or more of these objectives through previous study or experience. If so, you don't need to include them in your contract, but instead attach a separate slip to the contract indicating how you accomplished them and what evidence you have that you did accomplish them.

Any objectives in the syllabus that you have not already accomplished should be inserted in the contract. You don't need to follow the wording used in the syllabus; you may put the objectives into your own context—but if you do, indicate which objectives in the syllabus each of your objectives covers. Also, be sure that your objectives describe what you will *learn*, not what actions you will take. You may state them in whatever terms are most meaningful to you—content acquisition, behavioral performance, or directions of growth. But remember that they are *learning* objectives. Then, if you wish to contract for an *A*, specify what objectives (one or more) you propose to accomplish that will result in *distinguished* performance.

When you have finished listing your objectives, move over to the second column—"Learning Resources and Strategies," and describe how you propose to go about accomplishing *each* objective. Identify the resources (material and human) you plan to use and the strategies you will employ in making use of them. The more specific you are in describing the resources and strategies, the more helpful the instructor can be in making further suggestions. Think particularly of people in the university (especially fellow students in this course) and in the community who have expertness in the content area of the objective. For certain kinds of objectives, especially those involving skills or attitudes, the most appropriate resource may be your own experience (through a field project or experiment) and the most appropriate strategy may be analysis of that experience.

After completing the second column, move over to the third column—"Evidence of Accomplishment of Objectives," and specify what evidence you propose to collect. Perhaps the following examples of evidence will stimulate your thinking about what evidence you might accumulate:

| TYPE OF OBJECTIVE | EXAMPLES OF EVIDENCE |
|---|---|
| Knowledge | Reports of knowledge acquired, as in essays, examinations, oral presentations, audiovisual presentations; annotated bibliographies. |

| TYPE OF OBJECTIVE | EXAMPLES OF EVIDENCE |
|---|---|
| Understanding | Examples of utilization of knowledge in solving problems, as in action projects, research projects with conclusions and recommendations, plans for curriculum change, etc. |
| Skills | Performance exercises, video-taped performances, etc., with ratings by observers. |
| Attitudes | Attitudinal rating scales; performance in real situations, role playing, simulation games, critical incident cases, etc., with feedback from participants and/or observers. |
| Values | Value rating scales; performance in value clarification groups, critical incident cases, simulation exercises, etc., with feedback from participants and/or observers. |

After you have specified what evidence you will gather for each objective in the third column, move over to the fourth column—"Criteria and Means for Validating Evidence." For each objective, first specify what criteria you propose the evidence will be judged by. The criteria will vary according to the type of objective. For example, appropriate criteria for knowledge objectives might include comprehensiveness, depth, precision, clarity, authentication, usefulness, scholarliness, etc. For skill objectives, more appropriate criteria may be poise, speed, flexibility, gracefulness, precision, imaginativeness, etc. After you have specified the criteria, indicate the means you propose to use to have the evidence judged according to these criteria. For example, if you produce a paper or report, who will you have read it and what are their qualifications? Will they express their judgments by rating scales, descriptive re-

ports, evaluative reports, or how? One of the actions that help
to differentiate "distinguished" from "adequate" performance
in self-directed learning is the wisdom with which a learner
selects his or her validators. In this course, the appropriate
validators for certain objectives may be faculty members; for
other objectives it may be peers in the course (such as your
consultation team or your inquiry team); but for many objectives the most appropriate validators will be expert practitioners out in the community.

*Step 3.* After you have completed the first draft of your contract in the second session, you will participate in selecting a
consultation team of three or four peers. Each member of the
team will have a chance to review his or her contract with the
other members of the team in order to get their reactions and
suggestions.

Here are some questions you might ask them as a way of
getting optimal benefit from their help:

> Are the learning objectives clear, understandable, and
> realistic, and do they describe what you propose to
> learn?
>
> Can they think of other objectives you might consider?
>
> Do the learning strategies and resources seem reason-
> able, appropriate, and efficient?
>
> Can they think of other resources and strategies you
> might consider?
>
> Does the evidence seem relevant to the various objec-
> tives, and would it convince them?
>
> Can they suggest other evidence you might consider?
>
> Are the criteria and means for validating the evidence
> clear, relevant, and convincing?
>
> Can they think of other ways to validate the evidence
> that you might consider?

Between the second and third sessions you may wish to re-vise your contracts in the light of the inputs from your consultation team, and as a result of further study and further reflection. In any case, the contracts are due to be turned in to the instructor at the beginning of the third session. He or she will read them between the third and fourth sessions and return them to you with comments at the beginning of the fourth session. If the comments suggest further revisions, these should be submitted at the beginning of the fifth session.

*Step 4.* Between the fourth and the next-to-last session you will be carrying out the strategies, collecting the evidence, and having the evidence validated as specified in your contract. Thus, some of you will be engaging in group learning activi-ties during this period, while others of you may be engaging entirely in independent study, and still others will be doing some of both. At any time during this period you may find that your ideas about objectives, resources and strategies, and evidence are changing, and you may renegotiate your contract with the instructor accordingly.

*Step 5.* At the next-to-last session (usually the 13th or 14th) bring with you your contract in its final form, the evidence you have collected, and your evaluator's validations. The en-tire session will be devoted to your presenting this "package" to your consultation team and getting their reactions, sugges-tions, and—if called for in your contract—further validations.

This entire package is to be turned in to the instructor at the end of this session. He or she will return it to you, with com-ments and his or her judgments, at the last session. If further negotiation is required at this point because he or she cannot accept the evidence as fulfillment of the contract, it can take place at this session.

*Happy self-directed learning!*